Honey, let's buy a BOAT!

BOAT OWNERSHIP
Everything you wanted to know about buying *(and selling)*
a power boat but didn't know who to ask

Darren Finkelstein

Honey, let's buy a BOAT!
BOAT OWNERSHIP
Everything you wanted to know about buying (and selling) a power boat, but didn't know who to ask.

Proudly self-published in Australia by: Darren Finkelstein
M: 0418-379 369
E: darren@stkildaboatsales.com.au
Twitter: @thinkBoats
Facebook: darren.finkelstein
LinkedIn: Darren Finkelstein

www.letsbuyaboat.com.au

© Darren Finkelstein 2012

All rights reserved. No part of this publication may be reproduced, stored in a retrieval system, or transmitted in any form or by means, electronic, mechanical, photocopying, recording or otherwise, without the prior written permission of the publisher. Internal photos and content remains the property of their original owners and is used with their permission.

The International Standard Book Number (ISBN) assigned to this publication is:

Author: Finkelstein, Darren 1962 –
Title: Honey, let's buy a BOAT!
Subtitle: BOAT OWNERSHIP - Everything you wanted to know about
                buying (and selling) a power boat, but didn't know who to ask.
ISBN: 978-0-9873760-0-8
Subjects: Leisure and Recreation, Nautical, Sports and Games

Also available as an ebook: ISBN: 978-0-9873760-1-5

Author photo by: Gil Meydan
Cover Photo is used with permission from: Discover Boating USA and NMMA
Typesetting, front and back covers by: Susan Cooper, Sweetlip Design
Cover photo touch up by: Jeremy Finkelstein
Edited by: Stacey Dobis
Editorial assistance by: Ryan Kornhauser, Don Finkelstein, Suzi Finkelstein, Adam Finkelstein and Jeremy Finkelstein

Proudly printed in Australia by: Vivienne Kane - Excite Books, Prahran.
Safety and Weather information is used under Licence from: Transport Safety Victoria (TSV)
'Life Is Better With A Boat' – Is used with permission from:
Boating Industry Association of Victoria.

I dedicate this book to:

To all those people who have at any stage of their lives wished or dreamt about boat ownership and being on the water, but just didn't know how.

Life is full of people who are living the dream, who have made a choice to no longer spectate but to participate.

- Safe Boating Always -

Suzi my terrific wife of 27 years who continues to teach me new things every day.
Thanks for being flexible with re-arranging our lives so I could write.
Your unconditional support for my book project gave me the strength to see it through during the really tough times.
Your belief and encouragement for everything I do is wonderfully appreciated xxx

Jeremy and Adam, thank you for your advice, assistance and encouragement.
I love learning and growing with you guys.
Remember that when you put your mind to even the most bizarre ideas, add a little passion and some focus, you can make anything happen!
Remember to believe BIG, plan and never ever, give in.

Contents

Foreword
 - Andrew Griffiths, Australia's No 1 best-selling small business author   1

Introduction   3
 - What got me hooked?

1. **So you think you WANT a boat?**   11
 - Australia is the world's largest island, so why not!

2. **What to do with a Boat…**   19
 - A whole new world beyond land.

3. **Types of Boats.**   37
 - 20 choices to get you on the water.
 - Coolest boats in the world.

4. **Engines.**   89
 - Power to move.

5. **Boat Trailers.**   111
 - Limitless freedom.

6. **Where will you keep it?**   123
 - 7 storage ideas for stress free boating

7: **What's the cost of boating?**   143
 - Setting your boating budget.

8: **How to BUY a boat.**   167
 - Buying the right boat at the right price.

9: **Buyer Beware.**   191
 - Learning from others mistakes.

10: **How to SELL a boat.**   203
 - Proven ways to get a buyer's attention.

11: Safety and weather briefing. 235
- You're the Skipper, You're Responsible.

12: Top 10 Reasons to Buy a Boat. 259

Appendix

A: Glossary Of Terms 263
-What does all this boating stuff mean?

B: Compliant Boats 305
- The Australian Builders Plate and H.I.N explained.

C: Captain's Briefing 319
- Things to know.

D: Captain's Log 333
- Sample Forms.

Acknowledgments and References 347
- Thank You.
- References and Attributes to Content.

About The Author 355

Let's Keep In Touch 359

Foreword

Why on earth is a business author like me writing a foreword on a book about buying a boat? There is one very good reason - Darren Finkelstein is my hero. He has built a business around doing the things he loves, he lives large in every way and he sincerely believes that life is so much better with a boat.

I first met Darren at a workshop I was running on writing books. Darren was the cheeky bloke, sitting at the back of the room, and it took me a while to figure out why he wanted to write a book about buying a boat.

But then he stood up and started to share his ideas, his conviction and his passion, not just about buying a boat but about life and the need to live it fully. Then I understood exactly where he was coming from and I realised why his book was going to be fantastic.

When it comes to buying boats, no one has more knowledge than Darren. He spells it out, step by step in "Honey, let's buy a boat!", but I think he does a lot more. Darren's mission is to help people find that zest for life, to get families spending time outdoors, to be more active, healthy, laughing out loud and having a blast.

Whichever way you look at it, the world needs more Darren Finkelsteins. The fact that after you read this book you will want to buy a boat, and you will be much better equipped to do so, goes without saying. Most importantly though, you will want to step up and live a more rich and more rewarding life in every way, and that is simply spectacular.

Darren Finkelstein, you are my hero!

Andrew Griffiths
Australia's #1 Small Business Author, 11 books now sold in over 50 countries.

Introduction

What got me hooked on boating?

Make no mistake, I'm here to convince you that boats and boat ownership, is truly awesome and that *Life Is Better With A Boat*. Regardless of the SIZE of the boat, the idea of owning a floating oasis is not simply too good to be true, but the idea of boat ownership if done correctly, can make you both healthier and happier than ever before. I will provide you with information to overcome fears and common misconceptions about boat ownership, by challenging your beliefs and ideas about what boating is and what boating can do for you and your family, so be prepared.

Some of my earliest childhood memories are of the terrific times I had going fishing with my Dad and my two sisters, Debbie and Karen. Like so many other Victorians we escaped north from the cold of Melbourne's winter to Palm Beach on the Gold Coast every year during the May school holidays. We did all of the usual touristy things such as go to Sea World and visit the theme parks, but the real highlight for me was always doing plenty of fishing in nearby estuaries and creeks such as Tallebudgera.

I remember Dad deciding very early on that it was too hard to wake us up in the early hours of the morning to go fishing, so it was easier to simply go at night. After sunset we would pack our hand-lines, rods, bait

Introduction

and plenty of snacks and off to fish we'd go. Fishing off the bridge that crossed the creek was our favourite spot. We'd use the overhead street lights to attract the fish, much better than burley; it was free and didn't smell. It was the quietness of the night that Dad loved so much, he spent most of his time untangling our lines, baiting our hooks and getting the poisonous toad fish off the lines as my sisters would scream. For my sisters, Dad and I, it was great fun being together and it didn't bother us whether we caught plenty of fish or not. It was usually 1am before we packed up and went home.

Those times being with Mum, Dad and my sisters, now some 35 years ago and still today draw much family laughter and the stories constantly remind us all of how important spending quality time with your family is in one's life. I remember so clearly that the very first fish I caught was a little Bream, barely the right legal length. As it landed onto the jetty, I left the fish on my line and ran 1km back to our flat to see my parents and tell them of my victory. Mum jumped in the car and drove to the jetty where my first fish was still flapping about. We put it in the bucket and Mum drove home. Wow, armed with my first fish in the bucket, I was now hooked for life!

A few years later, a close friend of mine Paul suggested we go halves and buy a boat to go fishing and water-skiing. We had both done a bit of water-skiing on the river at the Carrera Ski School during a holiday where one of our friends was a part-time ski instructor. So Paul and I purchased a 1970's Caribbean Colt named 'Insatiable', with a Mercury 60hp Outboard engine on the back, from memory it cost us around $4,000. Paul was a sales rep in those days, so we used his company car to tow the boat. We skied behind the Colt and went fishing in Port Phillip Bay. Ahhh those were the days…

For many years we towed the Colt to the Hazelwood Pondage in Victoria's Latrobe Valley, to launch her in the hot waters of the pondage. I remember skiing in mid-July on the pondage with steam-rising from the warm

Introduction

water that was used to cool the turbines of the nearby Hazelwood Power Station. The air temperature would be about 8 degrees celsius as rain would fall - it felt like bullets as it hit our face which was numb because of the cold air and near freezing wind. With the wind-chill factor around 0 degrees celsius, nothing would stop us. Not even the time we launched the boat without the bung, only to fill the entire boat with water, lucky we had an operating bilge pump. What a great learning experience for a couple of teenagers, learning responsibility with their very first boat?

Paul and I traded-in the Caribbean Colt for a fire red 21ft Macho Ski Boat and with a Mercury 175hp Outboard on the back, we didn't know what to do with ourselves with so much acceleration. From a resting start, the 175hp Merc would just about pull our arms right out of our sockets. Now we would slalom and trick ski all summer long. Often visiting Yarrawonga or Lake Eildon, skiing all day and fishing at sunset, trying to catch ourselves a redfin or trout for dinner using paraveins and worms as bait.

Boating for me was a natural progression from fishing; it was a great learning experience about the water for us all. As 18-year-olds, boating taught us valuable life-lessons on topics such as; planning, maintenance, safety, costs, pride and responsibility for one's possessions. Boating can give us a wonderful opportunity to spend quality time in the outdoors; it would provide us with terrific memories that will remain with us for the rest of our lives.

To own a boat doesn't always require loads of money, so don't be scared off with what you think it may cost. For me I was lucky to have a few good jobs, which made boat ownership easier. My career highlight is having spent nearly 10 terrific years working at Apple during the Steve Jobs era', I was like a kid in a toy shop. I was fortunate enough to manage Apple's commercial markets and channel partners across the southern region of Australia. This meant I had full sales responsibility for Apple's key markets including; publishing, advertising, media, corporate & government, major accounts and retail. Part of my role required a lot of travel

Introduction

and I would regularly jet-off to the Apple HQ in Cupertino California with Aussie VIP's for Executive Briefings with Apple's senior Management Team including the likes of Steve Jobs and Apple's industrial design guru (Sir) Jonathon Ive. Pinch me please, I think I'm dreaming. What a buzz.... but boy what stress and pressure came with this lifestyle!

A few years on and a couple of kids later, my father in-law Hal, who is a real old-salt coming from a sailing background suggested that I could de-stress from my corporate world by boating, "get on the water and let your worries float away with the tide". Hal offered that if I were to buy a small 15ft half-cabin powerboat that he would pay for the annual storage of the boat at nearby St Kilda Marina. The marina was convenient to home and offered great access to the top end of the bay. This was conditional upon allowing him to go fishing by himself, with his mates and of course with his grandchildren. That was fine with me he could have used the boat anyway, regardless of whether he paid for the storage or not. But the boat got me down to St Kilda Marina in the first place, where I now spend much of my life.

Of course every boat owner knows that a bigger boat is always more appealing. I naturally was always looking for my next upgrade. After having had several boats stored in the marina over many years, the assistant marina manager Steve Mocellin said to me one day, "Why don't you work in the marine industry, given you just love boats and the water, so much?" Well...that's an interesting concept, so please read on...

With so many "wow" moments of my time at Apple, I remember the buzz of being a part of history when I was a member of the *National Road Show Team* that launched the colourful iMac to thousands of screaming people and the bewildered press. Looking back, I guess I feel part of the history of Apple, so that is pretty special!

Still with a yearning for boating and all things water, with my wife Suzi and our two boys Jeremy and Adam, we would hire houseboats on the Murray River with family friends and their kids, spending our days and

Introduction

nights enjoying the outdoors. We also had many return visits to one of Australia's best kept boating secrets; *Metung on the Gippsland Lakes* and would stay on the water at The Moorings resort, leaving the boat in one of the private berths. What terrific family holidays we shared with a boat. I remember towing our boat from Metung to Echuca over the top of Mt. Hotham. We have a great photo of the kids sitting in the boat under the main Hotham chair lift, which is a strange site. I clearly remember the smell of the burning rubber from our car's brakes, as we drove safely down the mountain heading to a houseboat holiday that we'd booked in Echuca.

It was 2001, September 11 in the USA and September 12 here in Melbourne, YES that day when the world changed forever – and so did it change my world too and cut me to the core. That morning after watching the terrible and tragic acts of terrorism to innocent people live on TV, I arrived at the Apple Melbourne office for work at 8.30am and was greeted by the Apple Australia CEO and my business manager, to be told I was being made redundant. What? Surely some mistake was made here, this couldn't happen to me. Ahhh, must be the wrong person.

Ouch, totally shell-shocked and completely surprised. The word 'redundant' is just way too hard to deal with! Filled with tears and white with shock, I jumped into my car and went down to the marina to play with my boat. Marinas are a very nice place to chill, to think and to try and clear your head. Working for a company like Apple in those days was bloody hard work, the battle with Microsoft wasn't being won by Apple, and so I was both physically and mentally destroyed and truly burnt out. The pressure for the delivery of numbers each quarter, for an American corporation that in the late 1990's and 2000's who wasn't doing so well was intense and relentless. Many years on, I see similarities of my time at Apple to being on a treadmill. When the speed is turned up, you just keep running and you can't even look around otherwise you'll fall off as the world passes you by. Forget smelling the roses, I was way too busy for that!

Introduction

Often I could be found at the marina or on my boat, nothing better than simply messing around with boats. Steve, the assistant marina manager, saw me on the day of my retrenchment and after I told him what had occurred and my longing to just stay at the marina all day, to play with boats. Steve smartly replied, *"Be-careful what you wish for, it might just happen."* Well done Steve, how right you were!

Armed with a payout, I took 12 months off to detox and heal my corporate scars. I kept my finger on the pulse of business by doing coaching sessions, helping friends fine-tune their businesses and spending time with my old Apple reseller channel.

It was now time for a "sea-change" *literally...* as a new chapter in my life begins. Having a passion and hobby for boating since being a kid, my terrific and always supportive wife, Suzi, begged me to get out of the bloody house.... and go to work (even for free) at St Kilda Marina, where my little fishing boat was stored. 'Just go and talk to someone down there, anyone, go and ask the boat sales guy', she said as I walked out the door.

Well Suzi was right (actually she is right about a lot of things, a lot of the time) I just need to listen more and believe, so I offered my sales and marketing services for free to the marina's boat sales office and after several weeks passed, a random opportunity arose that would change my life forever.

I was asked to buy the existing boat sales business called Steve Gow Marine (est. 1992) for a fair price as Steve the owner, wanted to quickly move overseas to marry his long-time girlfriend. As one door closes, another door opens, I immediately asked my long-time friend Andrew Rose, who also loved boating both power and sail, to be my business partner. Andrew had been crew of a charter boat throughout South-East Asia and sailed the east-coast of Australia delivering boats to their owners. The purchase contracts were signed on July 15, 2002 and St Kilda Boat Sales was born.

Introduction

Forget those so-called experts that say the best two days of owning a boat are- the day you buy it and the day you sell it! Those people simply did it wrong, if they've ever owned a boat at all.

This book answers all of your questions and outlines the process to make power-boat buying (*and selling*) within reach of everyone. Make no mistake; this book aims to convince you that boats and boat ownership are truly awesome and that *life is better with a boat*.

Boating is much more fun doing it together with your family and friends. *Guys*, do the hard-yards and your homework first! Don't think for a moment that the concept of the 'boys fishing boat' alone will cut it with the ladies. *Ladies*, make sure you get to spend plenty of time on the boat with your friends - remember a boat is not just a boy's toy! Boating is for everyone.

For us, it all started when we were kids, with a love of all things boating – the passion still continues today and passed down to our kids who too, have a love for the water as well.

"Be careful what you wish for, it might just happen."

- Safe Boating Always -

1

So you think you WANT a boat?

Australia is the world's largest island so why not!

Buying a boat has many perks including being called a number of things such as "boatie, old-salt, mariner or skipper," so if you are serious about owning a boat, get used to the term boatie! Also, the technical name for a boat is a 'vessel', but for simplicity sake I'm going to use the term *boat* everywhere within this book.

Much of the Australian population lives near the coast so we are always near the water. It seems the water for many of us has a kind of weird magical draw to her just like metal to a magnet, but with much more intrigue. To many aspiring *boaties*, it is not unusual to sit and gaze at the water with admiration, mixed with a touch of envy toward those who are already on the water and living the dream. For many bystanders, sadly there are feelings that will never be acted on, just simply stifled hoping they will soon go away. Sadly there are plenty of 'gonna's, should'aves and maybes', all spectators of life, just hanging around marinas.... so watch

So you think you WANT a boat?

your step. They will be staring at you, with that look of envy and longing in their eyes.

Living in this wonderful country of ours presents us with plenty of opportunity to safely experience and enjoy life near the water to the fullest. Most boaties will agree that boat ownership when done correctly, offers wonderful opportunities to spend quality time with family and friends away from life's distractions and in the outdoors. It doesn't get much better than that. It's all about having a better lifestyle.

For many, the bottom-line is that we all work way too hard usually in our pursuit of whatever is our motivation. For some; it's working to save for a deposit on a home, it's working to pay off the mortgage, it's working to put the kids through school, or it's working to pay off the car. We all understand this as we're all doing it, some so entrenched that they never get to smell the roses, never get to appreciate the journey and step back, for just a moment to take stock, regroup and refocus.

As I've reached my middle age (I've turned 50 at the time of writing this book) and look back at my own life's journey, I've realized that many people who start out with dreams, goals and desires, sadly don't always make it along the way. I've experienced this first-hand, saying good-bye to several friends taken from this earth too early. Some have taken a stumble and have never quite recovered, ill-health has stopped several in their tracks, whilst others just get side-tracked and never regain their focus and some sadly lose their way because they have lost their drive and don't even know why.

There are 800,000 owners of recreational boats that are registered here in Australia. It is these people who have, in most cases, had to defend their reasons for buying a boat from people who have stood in judgment of their decision. Can you believe it? Most of these judgmental people haven't ever owned a boat. Right from the outset as a boat owner you will need to stand ready to defend, justify and fight for your right to buy a boat, from those people who sadly can't see the value in being a *boatie*.

So you think you WANT a boat?

A space for you

Jodie Benveniste of www.parentwellbeing.com writes, "There's little doubt that parents who care for themselves are better parents. If you're stressed, preoccupied or exhausted, it's difficult to give children what we know they need – that is love, attention, consistency and boundaries. Our kids watch us more than they listen to us. We are role models for our children. If we come home from work irritable and ill tempered; then our children associate work with anger and annoyance. But if we come home from work, energized and engaged, then our children will look forward to work and a career."

Happy people are healthier, better workers, more popular, have better relationships, are resilient and live longer. You can add 10 years to your life by being happy. But, most of us get caught up in day to day irritations. We fume about the dirty clothes on the floor, the lid off the toothpaste, and the barely eaten dinner that we spent hours cooking. We believe if only our circumstances changed, we would be happier. If only we had a better job, a newer car, or a larger house in a better suburb, then our life would be better. With a boat, at last, you now have a place to go and even hide from the children to be temporarily substituted with the gentle lapping of water and the squawk of a sea-bird and a safe-haven. Ahh the serenity… Shhh quiet please, enjoy the silence…

In this sacred space there are no children to want something, no adults to want anything, just you and only you, if you so choose. Remember what having a choice is like? An enormous sense of freedom and a decent slice of independence all mixed together. That is exactly what you will find as a result of boat ownership, you will have a place to go requiring nothing at all from you, whatsoever, forever. Boat ownership gives so much back if you will just be open to receive all it has to offer.

Depending on your boat storage location, what you will soon discover is your boat can be a great place to go and relax without ever having to turn on the engines. Grab a good book, turn off your phone and enjoy the serenity. Ahh the serenity!

On most days at marinas all round Australia, it's not only the boat owners but their partners who come down to the marina to simply do nothing, but relax onboard their boats. Whether it's reading a good book, perhaps a newspaper, you may even take the laptop (given good broadband internet is available at minimal cost). The beauty of boat ownership means you can have your boat well-stocked with all of those nibbles, your favorite bottle of wine and a comfy cushion all in readiness for your afternoon sojourn to the land of floating-dreams.

For many years now boat owners have referred to their boat, whether it's is garaged or moored in the water at a marina or on a jetty, as being like a 'garden-shed' our Dads had when we were younger. Interesting comparison, but not all that surprising if you think about it for a moment.

In November 2011, Kerry McQueeney of www.dailymail.co.uk writes, "The humble garden-shed or as some say the man-cave, can help a man live longer... Pottering around 'lowers blood pressure and boosts self-esteem' the benefits could add years to a man's life."

It's long been cherished by men as a refuge to get on with some DIY, tackle a crossword, or even just for some peace and quiet away from the family. But, now it would seem the humble garden-shed has an even more valuable role; it could actually help men live longer, according to health experts.

For many men, the boat is a welcome retreat, I'm sure somewhere a health expert believes the boat could actually be a life-saver and the effects of boat ownership could add years to a man's life (as long as the man finds working on the boat relaxing and that in itself is good for their health.) Its clear there is link and a connection between a boat and the garden-shed. Surely the idea of going to your boat to relax and potter around using the time at the marina or in the garage, to prepare fishing rods, sort out the tackle box and tidy up the boat can be an attractive activity, especially those who have a highly stressful occupation, like I did.

Yes after you tidy her up, you can have an afternoon snooze, read the newspaper or a good book. For those that have a TV, perhaps watch the footy or the cricket before heading back home, refreshed and ready to be an active participant in family life, once again.

To do all of the above activities, without even turning on the engine, means you are not relying on the weather or relying on having anyone join you onboard, given you're not underway.

TIP: For those boaties located in areas where the water conditions are not brilliant and not always conducive to safe boating means when you're not underway you are more than likely cleaning-up and making your boat look great. Ultimately it's your boat and she will last longer and your resale value will be retained with regular maintenance.

Don't forget to bring your laptop down to the boat, as doing a few emails or a report for work is so much more appealing when you're sitting onboard your boat. It's amazing how much more productive you can be when you're not interrupted by your work colleagues regularly.

Family Time

How many times have you considered disconnecting the electricity at home, to get the kids to finally turn-off the bloody PlayStation, Xbox, Wii, computer, television - or even all of them at once? How frustrating is it dealing and managing the kids' usage of technology? Remember the

So you think you WANT a boat?

good ol' days when after school you went outside to ride bikes, kick the footy or climb trees, once I even got lost in a storm water drain. Huh, but not today.

Boating gets the kids off their behinds, it gets them outside and into the fresh air doing something that's healthy and they usually are the ones having the most fun. Perhaps you may want to ask them to bring a friend, perhaps their boyfriend or girlfriend or even both... Maybe they will be the ones who are actually driving the boat themselves, on a day out with their friends enjoying being on the water.

This photo is used with permission from Discover Boating USA

So you think you WANT a boat?

Boating brings added responsibility, it teaches great life-skills such as independence, common sense, planning, thinking ahead and initiative. It also means you now have another activity to share with your family and friends. It's nice to be able to have the broader family get involved and share the unique experience of boating with those that are close to you – and the extra hands on deck always helps too!

By delegating boating responsibilities and tasks that are shared across all the family members' means that everyone is working as a team, toward a common goal and can bring a combined sense of achievement to all participants, when things go to plan.

It's really interesting to listen to and watch a boating family talk about the tides, consider the winds and plan their voyage together. Family members that reverse the trailer, grab ropes when mooring and know how to turn-on the shore power are the ones who don't argue when they go boating. Everyone knows what is required and the skipper (usually Dad) feels an enormous relief when there are plenty of intuitive hands on deck to assist.

Just ask any adult to recall their earliest boating memories and it's those individuals who talk with big smiles on their faces about the wonderful times they shared together. All of those family holidays that most non-boating people would struggle to remember, but it's the boaties that seem to recall every holiday with intimate detail, much pride and enthusiasm. Today it is those very people who now have families of their own who are the one's buying a boat. It's those early memories that encourage and draw people to boating; many years later just like their parents did for them. What a wonderful legacy to pass onto the next generation and what a wonderful activity in which everyone can participate and can enjoy. Think about it, most sport or leisure activities are just for individuals or maybe as a member of a team, but rarely with the whole family to participate together.

So you think you WANT a boat?

> TIP: It's easy to find out what facilities are available near the water, just check with the local authorities, Google or drive by to investigate. There are many terrific restaurants on the water in and around every city and town in Australia. Maybe take your friends or family out to dinner by boat, it is a great way to enjoy the privileges of boat ownership and is a very memorable way to enjoy a night out. Your friends will talk about it forever.
>
> For those Melbournians out there, going to Etihad Stadium at the Docklands by boat, is a great way to avoid the traffic and show off a different face of the city to the family.

2

What to do with a boat

A whole new world beyond land.

Ski & Wake Boarding

Do you remember being taught how to water-ski by your parents or by one of their friends? Remember going to the family's favourite lake or river, trying to stand up on double skis for the first time it took hours. Then the realisation that you're actually standing up comes, only for you to fall down, hoping everyone on the boat saw you.

Why not give your kids and their friends the same opportunities you shared. How good is it to ski on really flat water and be able to carve those turns with the wind in your hair?

Perhaps you would rather try something a bit different…it's the modern technological influences of wake boarding that seems to capture the imagination of today's youth. It's all about getting air and hanging out on the

What to do with a boat

water, with music blaring, that draws our youth. The very cool lifestyle and persona of the wake boarder is perhaps the attraction. But, whatever it is, wakeboarding is a culture, not just a sport.

Water-skiing and wakeboarding doesn't involve sitting inside and watching TV or playing computer games. This is all about interacting with each other, being outdoors in the sunshine and communicating! Now that's all good!

Tubing

Maybe I'm just showing my age, but we used to all sit on the big banana-looking blow-up craft and get towed behind the boat. The object was to hold on as much as possible whilst the boat driver (usually Dad) pulled you through a whip, which was usually twice as fast as the boat was going. You would hold on for dear life and bounce up and down as you skimmed over the water surface, trying not to fall off as you hit the wash….

This photo is used with permission from my friends Hersh Burston, Leon Rothman, Jamie Ross and Joel Burston

Remember this? Well nothing has really changed too much. We have replaced a banana with a tube and now we hold on with as much strength as we can muster when Dad pulls into a whip!

Now you can even buy aerodynamically designed inflatable craft that enables you to get air and fly once the speed reaches a certain level. Due to the shape that creates lift (just like a plane's wing), you begin to fly over the water's surface, sometimes reaching the height of 10 or 15 feet in the air. Hold on as you touch back down to the water only to do it all again, and again…

"Life is Truly Better with a Boat."

Cruising

You would be surprised to learn that many of today's boats are modern day apartments on the water, and the marinas in which they are stored become the home away from home for many Australians as our love of the water fast becomes as important as our real houses.

Boat owners are choosing marina locations with as much care as a buyer of a house at an auction. Marinas are places to spend the weekend and time off, so location is fast becoming very important.

Depending on your boating location, most boats in marinas are used by their owners on weekends, with most country owners using their boats moored in city marinas as weekend city accommodation, just like holiday houses but with terrific water views. No body-corporate to deal with and a permanent swimming pool, that never needs cleaning.

The idea of heading down to the marina on a Friday night is very real. Pack your bags and stop by the bottle shop. Armed with your favourite bottle of red or a beer, head down to the marina, park your car and step aboard into a whole new world of fenders and navigation, not thinking about the office until Sunday night, when it's time to drive home. Take a look around the marinas on weekends, it will be full of boat owners all doing the same thing, chilling out and relaxing!

The long-distance cruising experience

A few years ago my business partner Andrew Rose and I were fortunate enough to build a very special relationship with a client of ours, Richard Mollard, who purchased from us a new Caribbean 40 Flybridge Cruiser.

Let's follow Richard's story. He is one very special customer whose dream voyage captured our interest and whose love of the water we wanted to share with you all, of course with Richard's approval.

Name:	Richard Mollard
Resides:	Brighton, Victoria
Age:	"Never you mind."
Marital Status:	Very happily married for many years with three grown-up children and several gorgeous grandchildren.
Occupation:	Successful businessman retired 2008
Why buy a boat:	Upon retirement, Richard's wife gave him a choice. She said, come and play bridge or perhaps take up lawn bowls with me. ... "I'm not playing lawn bowls," Richard said. So, Richard bought a big boat and named her NAVIS II instead.
Richard's decision:	Plan an on water voyage from Melbourne to Darwin via Cairns, on-board his own vessel. Catch loads of fish, eat well, drink well and

What to do with a boat

enjoy life. Have family and friends fly-in and join him for sections of the journey, otherwise he'd enjoy being aboard alone.

Motivation: Whilst Richard was mobile and in good health and whilst he was still able to dream of adventure and the sea, Richard felt this trip maybe his last, because of his age and being unsure of his future health - would enable him to close an important chapter in his life before he moved onto bridge and lawn bowls with his wife. Many years earlier, Richard had done a similar trip to this region on a much smaller boat named NAVIS and wanted to recreate that experience for just one more time.

Cairns to Lizard Island FNQ Aboard Navis II

My business partner Andrew Rose and I were invited guests of client Richard Mollard in June 2007 as we fished and explored our way through FNQ and the Great Barrier Reef in rough seas with; 30 knot (kts) winds which is equivalent to 55 km per hour from the South Easterly direction and with 2-3 metre swells. Very uncomfortable to say the least.

Here is a part of our trip diary aboard Navis II, a 2006 Caribbean 40 Flybridge Cruiser as we journey from Yorkeys Knob Marina in Cairns to Lizard Island via Cooktown and a few uninhabited islands and reefs along the way.

What to do with a boat

This photo of Richard Mollard in the galley of Navis II, cooking up a storm, is used with permission from the private collection of Darren Finkelstein

Sunday — Cairns to Cooktown

SE 20kts, 2m swells behind us, as we make our way towards Cooktown some 200kms due north. En route, we pass Mission Beach, Palm Cove and Port Douglas. We trek pass the wonderful Cape Tribulation surrounded by the heritage-listed Daintree National Park. Following Captain Cook's famous passage in 1770, we navigate the last 2 hours of the voyage on our Raymarine C120 (GPS, Chart Plotter, Echo-Sounder, Radar and Auto-Pilot) as it's dark and overhead cloud cover prevents ambient light from the moon and stars. We navigate into the well-lit shipping channel and head east towards Cooktown along the famous Endeavour River.

We arrive into Cooktown, safe and sound, at 9pm and quickly make it to the 1770 restaurant for dinner and a cold beer before heading off to bed aboard our very comfortable Caribbean 40 Flybridge Cruiser.

Monday — Cooktown to Lizard Island

SE 30kts and 2-3m swell is again behind us, as we make our way north towards Lizard Island some 45nm. Rainsqualls sweep in, stir up the sea and move on... We set our rods and lures and trawl much of the way. We are in the shipping channel and sometimes get the feeling we are in peak hour traffic back in Melbourne. We head towards the twins; North & South Direction Islands as we get our first hit on the lines. The reels roar as line peels off and the bugger has got away. This happens again shortly after, much to our disappointment.

We finally reach our destination and seek the protection of Watson Bay at Lizard Island. We find a public mooring buoy and enjoy the sites of the heritage-listed National Marine Park. We use the crane on the bow of Navis II (aka: Davit) which we installed on the vessel to launch our Quicksilver Tender powered by an effective Mercury 8hp and head ashore. The beach is wonderful, the sun is shining and we are in tropical paradise. We head to the (in)famous Marlin Bar, empty with just the three of us and G (Graham aka: Big G, Super G, G Banger, Big Fella), our 6'4 New Zealand born professional deckhand.

This photo of Navis II anchored at Watsons Bay Lizard Island, is used with permission from the private collection of Darren Finkelstein

What to do with a boat

On the walls of the bar are the famous catches of Marlins, overhead is a 1,100kg monster, hanging from the ceiling. Richard explains the history of the region as we visit the last remains of the famous Mrs Watson homestead. Richard is very well read on this area, and a keen historian. He is like a talking Google, but with loads of personality. Overnight, the Caribbean 40 offers plenty of room on-board for all of us as we sleep like babies against the gentle lapping of water.

How nice is this…

Tuesday — Lizard Island to Cape Bedford

SE 30kts 2-3m swell again, but this time we are punching straight into it. Interesting to note that even in these harsh conditions, we were travelling at a brisk, yet comfortable speed of 16kts and averaging only 45L per engine/hour. We make our way south towards the protection of Cape Bedford some 25nm. Rainsqualls sweep in, stir up the sea and move on as we punch straight into the slop, waves constantly breaking over the Flybridge .

We set our rods, lures and trawl much of the way with no success. It seems several other mariners have decided on the same thing as we share the protection of the Cape with a couple of yachts and a few local trawlers. Andrew and Richard launch the Tender and head to shore amongst the mangroves to catch a Barramundi for dinner. Darren stays on-board with G, as we try to our luck from the comfort of the Caribbean 40 and her enormous cockpit.

After several hours fishing and many bites later, we catch a few small fish including: a reef shark, hammerhead shark and seagull (that's a funny sight). Richard and Andrew return without dinner, so I guess it's steaks from the freezer on the BBQ for us all.

Wednesday — Cape Bedford to Hope Island

SE 30kts 2-3m swell and yet again we are punching straight into it. Still heading south, today towards the protection of Hope Island some 30nm. Rainsqualls sweep in, stir up the sea and move on as we punch straight into the slop. Waves constantly break over the Flybridge as we pound south.

Like yesterday, we set our rods and lures and trawl much of the way via coral reefs, but this time with success!! Andrew fights hard with a 25kg Giant Trevally and lands her. What a huge fish — we take the usual photos and set her free. We detour via another reef to bottom bounce, catching loads of nice sized reef fish including: Reef Cod, Red Emperor, Sweet Lip and Coral Trout. We only keep tonight's dinner and release the rest safely, to live another day.

This photo of Happy Hour at sunset usually sees the opening of a nice bottle of Merlot from Richards on-board Cellar (specially converted part of the engine bay) and Richard with a Monte Christo No 3 Cigar. This photo is used with permission from the private collection of Richard Mollard.

What to do with a boat

We make a beeline straight for the protection of the uninhabited Hope Island. Again, it seems several other mariners share our idea and we find a couple of yachts and a few local trawlers.

We go ashore, Richard has a fish and a snooze, while the rest us have a swim and snorkel in the clear blue waters of this peaceful Island.

SE 30kts 2-3m swell again, as we make our way south towards the protection of the Low Island group some 30nm. Rainsqualls sweep in, stir-up the sea and move on as we punch straight into the slop. Waves constantly break over the Flybridge as we pound south. We set our rods and lures and trawl much of the way via coral reefs, but this time no success! So we head towards the Bat Reef area, the location of the famous Wildlife Warrior — Steve Irwin's — tragic death.

We bottom bounce for hours, catching loads of nice sized reef fish including: Reef Cod, Red Emperor, Sweet Lip and Coral Trout. Again, we only keep tonight's dinner and release the rest to live another day. Arriving at Low Island at 4pm, we admire the lighthouse and this picturesque area. G, our decky, knows the skipper of the trawler moored nearby and hops in the Tender to visit. G comes back with a bag of fresh prawns, which make a wonderful appetiser — washed down by the usual quantity of beers — at Beer O'clock of course.

That evening as we proudly eat our catch, we are entertained by the many reef sharks circling our Caribbean 40, to fight for our prawn tails that we are feeding them. What a sight...

Next morning, we visit the island to explore the lighthouse and met the lighthouse keeper, Steve. An interesting guy who lives on the island with his wife and very young family, and all that serenity!

Friday — Low Island to Cairns

SE 30kts 2-3m swell yet again, as we make our way South towards home some 30nm, enough already with the wind... Here we go again... Rainsqualls sweep in, stir-up the sea and move on as we punch straight into the slop. Waves constantly break over the Flybridge, as we pound south. A quick detour on our return leg, sees us bottom bounce, once again. We are happily catching loads of nice sized reef fish at the beginning, and then she dried-up and without a bite, we returned to Cairns and packed-up the rods for this trip. The heavens opened again for yet another rain squall and we arrived safely back at Yorkeys Knob in the afternoon, returning to Cairns six days later, having covered a total trip distance of 280 nautical miles.

G washed down the boat whilst the rest of us have a long shower, removing salt from everywhere. Dinner at the marina Friday night, followed by watching the AFL on the boat live... What a bonus...

Saturday — Cairns

After breakfast on the very cosmopolitan esplanade of Cairns, we went shopping for the kids. Andrew's kids; Jett and Harley will be really happy with their toys, even though we hunted for hours trying to find them police cars. The smile on the kid's faces will be worth the hassle of shopping for toys in Cairns.

Both Andrew and I were thrilled by Richard's invitation to join him, Richard is a very successful businessman and proud grandfather with a strong 'Flinders Lane' heritage that he shared with us. Richard was kind enough to share his boating dream and enjoyment with us.

We are stronger for having this journey behind us. We understand firsthand the Caribbean 40's wonderful sea-handling capabilities and appreciate the ocean and her powers. Richard and G also headed from Cairns

What to do with a boat

to Darwin in August - October 2007 and we have posted Richard's stories and pictures on our website for all to share.

Go to: www.stkildaboatsales.com.au

Richard thanks for taking such great care of us.

God Bless You.

This photo taken in October 2006 of Richard Mollard's brand new Caribbean 40 Flybridge Cruiser NAVIS II being loaded at Sandringham Yacht Club in Melbourne for the road-trip to Brisbane is used with permission from the private collection of Darren Finkelstein

What to do with a boat

Fishing

There's fishing and there is FISHING.

It is a topic that triggers such passion and emotion that it's very difficult for me to capture the essence of fishing. So to show total respect to the die-hard fisho's out there, I won't even try.

Fishing is a part of the male psyche, it's a part of our primeval "hunter-gatherer" thing. It's a bloke thing, but equally it's a girl thing and it's a kid thing. Fishing is NO longer gender specific since all the ladies realise exactly how much fun the blokes were having and decided to join in.

Fishing is for everyone, regardless of age, gender or religion.

Suffice to say you can, and should go and buy terrific fishing books, DVDs, tutorials and guides, read up and go and catch that dream fish by yourself, with family or with your mates! Enjoy the best that life has to offer and experience the outdoors as you never have before.

> **TIP:** Go fishing with your children and if you don't have a child, then take your nephew or niece. If you don't have relatives, then take a friend's children, but whatever you do you MUST go fishing just once with a child. Simply to watch their face as they reel in their very first fish. It's truly a sight to behold and an experience that you and the child will remember forever!

Top 10 Reasons to Go Fishing

There is no need to convince the thousands of Aussies of the benefits of fishing, but if for some reason, you do need a little convincing, below is a great list of 10 good examples that I want to share with you.

The list compiled might just offer you an excuse to call in sick to work or leave those "to-dos" for another weekend so you too can spend a day fishing.

1. **Contribute to Conservation:** Anglers put their money where their mouth is and are passionate about the environment. By purchasing fishing licenses, they themselves have agreed to fund many of the wildlife and conservation programs that exist in Australia. They also contribute to education programs, and facility upgrades. Anglers are also acutely aware of the importance of clean water and air and pride themselves on protecting and preserving our environment, natural communities, and valuable habitat.

2. **Stress Relief:** Ask most anglers why they enjoy spending time in the outdoors and you're likely to hear the word "freedom". Spending a day afield casting for trout on a cool mountain stream or fishing for Trout on a pond helps to release us from our highly stressful, everyday environment. Nothing brings on the sense of being alive and helps to rebuild our personal reserves like a day spent interacting with nature.

3. **Social Bonding:** Sharing a fishing experience helps strengthen relationships with family and friends. It also offers a person the chance to give back to society through mentoring others in the pleasure and importance of being good stewards of our natural resources.

4. **Supports Wildlife and Fisheries Management:** Angling is an important wildlife management tool. For more than 100 years anglers have helped to contribute to wildlife and fisheries management ef-

forts by helping to set seasons and creel limits. Wildlife populations of most fish species remain stable and in some cases flourish, a far cry from a decade ago when many species suffered from over-harvesting and the ill effects of pollution. Anglers also have a vested interest in and support many efforts to preserve and protect all species and the environment — all the while helping to increase biodiversity.

5. **Health Benefits:** More than fifty percent of Australians are overweight. Being outside and being active helps to make you feel better and encourages a healthier way of life. Driving to your local grocery store and fast food restaurant might be convenient, but fishing can also help you burn those unwanted calories, increase the quality of your lifestyle, and add years to your life. Eating fish is good for you, just ask your doctor.

6. **Recreation:** Having a bad day of fishing still beats a day in the office or tending to house chores. Fishing is simply fun and whether you enjoy trolling for stripers or outwitting a weary brook trout with a hand-tied fly that imitates an insect the size of a pin head, there is much enjoyment to be had by all.

7. **Self-Fulfilment:** Fishing offers you the chance to improve your self-esteem through respect for the environment, mastering outdoor skills and achieving personal goals. Fishing can also play an important role in one's personal and social development. Fishing is a lifetime skill and activity that can be enjoyed at any age. Just ask a youngster who reeled in their first fish how much fun fishing can be.

8. **Boost to the Economy:** Australian anglers generate millions in state revenues and directly support thousands of jobs, giving an economic boost that any state government would be pleased with.

9. **Fishing for Food:** Wild fish are low in fat and cholesterol and high in protein. In fact, many health organizations recommend a regular diet of fish. Besides it's a lot more challenging to catch that plate of

fresh fish than to stroll endlessly down a supermarket aisle if you decide to keep your catch.

10. **The Thrill:** Fishing has a way of fulfilling an age-old need of pursuing and catching. The thrill lies in the challenge, such as stalking an elusive Marlin, Barramundi or Big-Red Snapper. But there are many who will be quick to profess that it's not the catching of fish that's important, but the immeasurable life lessons that you will experience along the way.

Corporate Entertaining

Building long-term relationships is a basic fundamental of business today. Taking out clients on your boat for a day's social fishing, maybe a quiet drink and lunch, or just a cold beer is a great way of breaking down barriers. Finding that edge ahead of your opposition may just enable you to close the sale before someone else does.

Corporate entertaining on your boat opens a world of opportunity that is no longer a business tool for the mega-rich, but available to all.

Many boat owners hire a skipper for a few hours so they can concentrate on being a great host and let someone else drive your boat. You can at least have a drink without the worry of being over the alcohol limit!

What to do with a boat

TIP: You may even decide to take a boat load of clients to a sporting match if your venue is next to where you can moor your boat. In Melbourne the Etihad Stadium at Docklands is only 200 meters from the water's edge. So going to the AFL, soccer, cricket, rugby or a concert in your boat and then afterward going to a nearby restaurant for dinner is very easy to arrange and is an experience that your customers will never forget. After all, how many times would they do this? Forget the traffic and finding a decent car park. Hire a Skipper, so you don't have to worry about it and can drink and enjoy the event.

When we talk corporate and business entertainment, you along with most business people do think "tax deductibility". You need to be very careful and ask your financial advisor for advice first before buying that million-dollar dream-boat or any boat for that matter.

Past experience suggests that claiming tax deductibility on a boat purchase usually draws the attention of the Australian Taxation Office. So if the boat is not built to survey, if it is not driven by a qualified skipper with Master 5 rating, and if you don't have a business plan whose sole-objective is to make profits from chartering, then you can forget it!

Most boats you see at marinas around Australia will be built for recreational purposes only and not commercial, as most leading recreational boat manufacturers don't make a commercial vessel to survey standards.

Commercial boats are built to survey and it's very costly and sometimes impossible to convert a recreational boat to survey standard!

Get advice from your accountant or financial advisor and be very careful.

3

Types of boats

20 choices to get you onto the water

Deciding which boat is right for you and your family may be the hardest part of your new boating experience. There are many different types, styles and engines to choose from. However, if sail boats are your thing, I'm very sorry, but my years of experience and interest are within recreational power boats. If you are looking for information on sailing it would be best to consult an expert or perhaps talk to patrons at your local yacht club.

Armed with my recreational powerboat hat firmly on my head, this chapter has been written to help you narrow down your boat selection choices by giving you a general overview of the different types of recreational power boats available in today's Australian market.

Hull Construction - Fibreglass vs. Aluminium

What does it all mean?

There are several choices of materials from which your boat will be made. About 90% of modern styles of self-planing trailerable and cruiser type boats are made from just two basic materials; aluminium and fibreglass.

Both were developed in the late 1950s, replacing plywood or "bondwood" as the favored boat building materials. The Spooner family of International Marine (the makers of Caribbean Boats) are the true industry pioneers here in Australia. In fact, Arch Spooner in circa 1958 at Caribbean Gardens in the Melbourne suburb of Scoresby was the first person to introduce fibreglass into boat building.

The advantage of the new materials, especially fibreglass, was the manufacturer's ability to produce identical boats quickly from moulds, this was far more efficient and with relatively unskilled labour. As you can imagine, this revolutionised recreational powerboat manufacturing, opening the door for the establishment of many new companies, as well as giving builders the ability to experiment with different hull types and configurations.

Aluminium Boats

Alloy boats or "Tinnies" as they are known throughout Australia, are favourites with small boat buyers and inland, estuary fishermen. Remarkably, up to 90% of boats in the 0 - 4.5 m size class are manufactured from aluminium. The majority of these craft are built using sheets of relatively light weight aluminium (1.2 - 3.0 mm) which are "pressed" to provide rigidity and strength. Pressed aluminium boats are most popular in sizes up to around 5.0 m, and have a number of advantages over fibreglass boats. They are light, durable and require less horsepower and in the smaller sizes usually less expensive than fibreglass. Conversely, they are also quite hard riding and noisy, and they rattle and vibrate underway. They don't have the practical working life of most fibreglass as they suffer from electrolysis or cracking after years of pounding over the water. In addition to the pressed alloy boat builders, there are specialist manufacturers of what are called "plate" alloy boats. Plate alloy boats are generally considered to be stronger and more durable (albeit much heavier) because they are built using thicker alloy sheet (up to 6.0 mm).

Plate alloy boats can usually be identified by their smooth hull finish along the topsides, as opposed to the paneled look of the lighter weight pressed alloy models.

Fibreglass Boats

Fibreglass or just 'glass boats' as they are commonly known, have been really popular in Australia and fibreglass trailer boats are most popular in sizes above 5.0 m in length. On the used boat market, there is plenty of top quality brands available including: Caribbean, Streaker and Haines. Fibreglass boats are easier to build than alloy boats, but more importantly, fibreglass boat designers are able to create much more sophisticated and softer riding hull shapes. As a general rule, fibreglass boats also handle better through turns, are sportier in appearance, move through the water much quieter, are more attractive and more luxuriously fitted out.

A disadvantage of the fibreglass trailer boat is its weight, at least when compared with a pressed alloy boats under 5.5m in length. Fibreglass boats are often heavy and need more power for good performance and demand a more powerful tow vehicle. Contrary to wide belief, fibreglass boats are considerably tougher than aluminium. Simply because fibreglass doesn't rip or tear as aluminium can do. If you were to hit rock or a submerged object, you are less likely to hole than if in aluminium. Also the bounding caused by trailer travel and choppy seas, does not weaken structurally fibreglass as it does that of aluminium. You do have to be careful on the launch ramp or near rocks etc., to avoid cracking and gouging the gelcoat or outer skin of the fibreglass.

These days it is not uncommon to see many 30 year old fibreglass boats still happily working the waterways, most boaties know of them as the early models of Bertram, which were made by the crew at International Marine under licence.

Types of boats

Before you begin to shop for your new or used boat, it's important to think about these key factors:
1. What activities do you want to do?
2. What are your expectations?
3. Where are you going to store it?
4. What type of budget do you have allocated?

The key factors above will allow you to quickly establish the correct boat for your particular circumstance. The good news is there's a boat for every need and budget. To assist the process, consider the following categories. You might decide your particular boating need, crosses over into several other categories below whist this is very common, try to truly get your priorities into perspective.

What are your must haves and those that would be nice to have? This will allow you to focus on what's really important. We've asked the big question in my first chapter; So you think you want a BOAT? Now the next question becomes what sort...

For simplicities sake, here are some very broad and common uses for a boat that we will work with:
- **Water Skiing/Wake Boarding**
    o Social (with family and friends)
    o Competition (clubs and tournaments)
- **Fishing/Diving**
    o Social (with family and friends)
    o Sport (serious or recreational)
    o Competition Game Fishing (clubs and tournaments)
- **Cruising**
    o Day cruising (social only)
    o Overnight (weekender or holiday house)
    o Long-range (east-coast voyage)

Take a look at the wide selection of boat types available to decide what's best for you.

Different Types of Boats

Some of the information I have referenced in this chapter can be directly attributed to the good folk at Discover Boating USA and www.discoverboating.com, which is one of the most wonderful online tools available today for boat buyers, boat sellers and boat owners alike.

Types of boats

PERSONAL WATERCRAFT (PWC or Jet Skis)

PWC
This photo is used with permission from my friends:
Hersh Burston, Leon Rothman and Joel Burston

Types of boats

Personal Watercraft is popular among boaters seeking thrills, adventure and fun.

PWCs offer state-of-the-art features allowing you to safely and comfortably explore the waterways. Whether you're riding solo or taking the family on an adventure, PWC owners can enjoy a variety of activities, ranging from touring rides to water sports such as tubing, water-skiing and fishing. PWCs are easy to store, maintain and transport, and are quite affordable.

Many models have on-board storage, adjustable handlebars for comfortable steering, a re-boarding step to help you back on-board after a refreshing dip, tow hooks for skiers and wake boarders — and some models even have cruise assist for longer tours on the water.

Technical Information

Hull Construction -	Fibreglass
Minimum Length -	8 feet (2.43m)
Maximum Length -	13 feet (3.96m)
Maximum Capacity -	3 people
Trailerable -	Yes
Propulsion Type -	Jet Engine
Sleeping -	No
Price Guide (brand new) -	A$12,000 to A$22,000 depending on engine and option selection

Popular brand names available in the Australian market include: Sea-Doo, WaveRunner, Kawasaki and Honda.

INFLATABLES

RIB
This photo is used with permission from: Mercury Marine

Types of boats

Two categories of inflatable boats include roll-up inflatables or rigid-hull inflatable boats (RIBs), they both share key benefits distinguishing them from other types of boats. These boats are suitable for saltwater and freshwater fishing and water sports. Typically, they are used as a Tender to a larger vessel used for transporting passengers to shore or onto other boats. Sometimes they are referred to as Dinghies.

Technical Information

Hull Construction -	Hypalon, Neoprene or PVC
Minimum Length -	8 feet (2.43m)
Maximum Length -	30 feet (9.14m)
Maximum Capacity -	6 people
Trailerable -	Yes
Propulsion Type -	Outboard engine, Sterndrive engine, jet engine, manual power (oars)
Sleeping -	No
Price Guide (brand new) -	A$3,000 to A$70,000 depending on engine and option selection

Popular brand names available in the Australian market include: Zodiac, Quicksilver, Amanzi and Brig.

Types of boats

DINGHIES

DINGHY
This photo is used with permission from: Quintrex

Types of boats

Dinghies are small boats similar to RIB's that can be carried or towed by larger vessels such as: Houseboats, Sports boats, Flybridge Cruisers or Motor Yachts. Dinghies are used when the mother ship cannot venture into the shallows or in ports where it can be difficult to manoeuver a larger vessel. They also make good companion boats for camping trips or for fishing smaller waters.

Most modern dinghies have either a rigid hull made of fibreglass, aluminium, or marine plywood or an inflatable hull made from rugged, coated fabrics. Oars and small outboard engines are the principle methods of propulsion.

Technical Information

Hull Construction -	Fibreglass and Aluminium
Minimum Length -	5 feet (1.24m)
Maximum Length -	12 feet (3.65m)
Maximum Capacity -	5 people
Trailerable -	Yes
Propulsion Type -	Outboard engine or manual power (oars)
Sleeping -	No
Price Guide (brand new) -	A$12,000 to A$30,000 depending on engine and option selection

Popular brand names available in the Australian market include: Quintrex, Ally Craft, Stacer and Savage

Types of boats

BASS, BREAM or BARRA BOATS

BARRA BOAT
This photo is used with permission from: Quintrex

Types of boats

Bream or Barra Boats are called Bass Boats in the USA. They have low, sleek profiles and are built to fish with two or three anglers on-board. Tournament style boats are more than 18-feet (5.48m) long with between 150hp to 250hp engines.

For casual angling and buddy tournaments, aluminium boats from 16ft (4.87m) to 18 feet (5.46m) fitted with 25hp to 150hp outboard engines are more common. Live-wells to keep the catch alive are mandatory, as is an electric trolling motor on the bow (front of boat). Some have hulls with flat bottoms to enable shallow water access.

Technical Information

Hull Construction -	Fibreglass vs. Aluminium
Minimum Length -	16 feet (4.87m)
Maximum Length -	25 feet (7.62m)
Maximum Capacity -	5 people
Sleeping -	No
Price Guide 9brand new) -	A$25,000 to A$50,000 depending on engine and option selection

Popular brand names available in the Australian market include: Quintrex, Ally Craft, Stacer and Streaker Boats.

Honey, let's buy a BOAT!

Types of boats

RUNABOUTS

RUNABOUT
This photo is used with permission from: Streaker Boats

Types of boats

Versatile boats used primarily for fishing and diving are made either from fiberglass and called a Runabout or made from aluminium and lovingly referred to in Australia, as a Tinnie.

If you've been lured to boating by a love of the outdoors, an all-purpose cruising, skiing, tubing, fishing or dive boat like a Runabout is an ideal choice. Built for versatility, these boats can be used in both saltwater and freshwater. They are designed to navigate many different types of waterways so you can pursue many different species of fish. All-purpose fishing and dive boats typically feature live wells, rod lockers, a bow (front) or transom (aft or rear motor mounting position) trolling motor and powerful outboard motor. Open areas give good options for dive tank and water ski, wake board storage.

Technical Information

Hull Construction -	Fibreglass and Aluminium
Minimum Length -	8 feet (2.43m)
Maximum Length -	20 feet (6.09m)
Maximum Capacity -	5 people
Trailerable -	Yes
Propulsion Type -	Outboard engine or manual (oars)
Sleeping -	No
Price Guide (brand new) -	A$30,000 to A$60,000 depending on engine and option selection

Popular brand names available in the Australian market include: Caribbean, Quintrex, Streaker Boats, Haines Signature, and Savage.

Types of boats

ALUMINUM FISHING BOATS (TINNIE)

TINNIE
This photo is used with permission from: Quintrex

Types of boats

Small lightweight and durable trailer boats made of aluminium and in Australia lovingly referred to as a Tinnie. Tinnies are often used for both salt and freshwater fishing. Generally a very simple craft, featuring riveted or welded aluminium hulls and bench seating, they can be operated in fish-friendly places - shallow water, coves, inlets (areas not many other boats can reach). Powered primarily by outboard engines, this type of boat offers both tiller and remote steering options. If you're an outdoor enthusiast looking for even more versatility, you may want to consider a flat bottom car topper punt style of boat.

Punts are flat-bottomed aluminium, multi-purpose fishing, camping and hunting boats featuring bench seats and a simple flat transom. Also known as car toppers, they can be easily lifted on top of the car and secured by roof racks or rope. A 6 x 3 metre trailer also can easily transport them. Powered by a small to moderate tiller-steered outboard, Jon boats offer easy maintenance, low cost and are nearly indestructible.

Tinnies are the most affordable and simplest way to get on the water, they are ideal for a wide variety of on-water, family friendly activities which include fishing and cruising.

Technical Information

Hull Construction -	Aluminium
Minimum Length -	8 feet (2.43m)
Maximum Length -	24 feet (7.31m)
Maximum Capacity -	8 people
Trailerable -	Yes
Propulsion	Type - Outboard engine
Sleeping -	No
Price Guide (brand new) -	A$5,000 to A$40,000 depending on engine and option selection.

Popular brand names available in the Australian market include: Quintrex, Ally Craft, Stacer and Savage.

Types of boats

BOW-RIDERS

BOW RIDER
This photo is used with permission from: Streaker Boats

Types of boats

These are quickly becoming one of the most popular boats in the Runabout/Sportboat category, thanks to the spacious seating in their open bow (front) area. Swim platforms at the stern (back) are handy for swimming, donning skis or just dangling toes in the water when at anchor. Sterndrive power plant is the norm for the larger length Bow Riders, but Outboard engines are becoming increasingly popular in the 15 to 21 foot range.

Bow Riders can be pure boating fun depending on the boating location you've chosen. A word of caution, due to the openness of this type of boat, both sun and wind protections are minimal, so consider this when weighing up your options.

Technical Information

Hull Construction -	Fibreglass and Aluminium
Minimum Length -	16 feet (4.87m)
Maximum Length -	30 feet (9.14m)
Maximum Capacity -	12 people
Trailerable -	Yes
Propulsion Type -	Outboard engine, Sterndrive engine, jet engine
Price Guide (brand new) -	A$35,000 to A$100,000 depending on engine and option selection

Popular brand names available in the Australian market include: Sea Ray, Bayliner, Four Winns, Caribbean, and Streaker Boats.

Types of boats

CUDDY or HALF CABINS

HALF CABIN
This photo is used with permission from: St Kilda Boat Sales

Types of boats

Perfect for family boating and small groups of four to eight passengers, Cuddy Cabins are nimble and manoeuverable like Bow-Riders, but have an enclosed deck over the bow, offering great protection and additional open storage.

A Half Cabin boat has the additional bulk-head and door to offer privacy, a cosy sleeping area, secure storage and in some models even a full-flush toilet (or porta-potty), sink and sometimes with limited cooking facilities. The lockable undercover area is ideal for family boating offering shade and protection from both the sun and the wind.

Available options such as a sun-pad, swim platform and towline hook make them ideal for a wide variety of uses including: family cruising, fishing, diving, skiing, tubing and wakeboarding. This type of boat is available in both fiberglass and aluminium construction.

Technical Information

Hull Construction -	Fibreglass and Aluminium
Minimum Length -	14 feet (4.27m)
Maximum Length -	24 feet (7.31m)
Maximum Capacity -	8 people
Trailerable -	Yes
Propulsion Type -	Outboard engine, Sterndrive engine or jet engine
Sleeping -	Yes very basic, effectively for 2 people camping style

Price Guide (brand new) – A$35,000 to A$160,000 depending on engine and option selection. Popular brand names available in the Australian market include: Caribbean, Haines Signature, Streaker Boats, Stabicraft and Barcrusher.

Types of boats

PONTOON BOATS

PONTOON
This photo is used with permission from: Ski Force Australia

Types of boats

Pontoons' hallmark feature is comfort on the water with living room-like couches, BBQ's, lounges and swivel seats that beckon boaters to sit back, put up their feet and enjoy the breeze, the sunset or whatever they want on the water. Pontoons can offer slow and lazy rides and are economically priced with smaller engines. When equipped with higher horsepower, they offer relaxation and speed, some with power for skiing and tubing as well.

Technical Information

Hull Construction -	Aluminium
Minimum Length -	16 feet (4.87m)
Maximum Length -	30 feet (9.14m)
Maximum Capacity -	15 people
Trailerable -	Yes
Propulsion Type -	Outboard engine, Sterndrive engine
Sleeping -	No
Price Guide (brand new) -	A$15,000 to A$60,000 depending on engine and option selection

Popular brand names available in the Australian market include: Sylvan

CENTER CONSOLES

CENTRE CONSOLE
This photo is used with permission from: St Kilda Boat Sales

Types of boats

These open freshwater and saltwater fishing boats are built to take rough offshore waters in pursuit of ocean fish like Grouper, various Billfish, Tuna, Mahi-Mahi and other migrating species of big game. A bait-well is necessary to keep live bait on-board and fish lockers should be insulated to keep fish iced. An aluminium and canvas Bimini Top provides shade and rod storage. Gunwale rod holders, Outriggers and other sport fishing gear are common fittings.

Technical Information

Hull Construction -	Fibreglass and Aluminium
Minimum Length -	18 feet (5.18m)
Maximum Length -	28 feet (8.53m)
Maximum Capacity -	7 people
Trailerable -	Yes
Propulsion Type -	Outboard and Sterndrive Engine
Sleeping -	Yes, very basic in some makes, effectively for 2 people camping style.
Price Guide (brand new) -	A$40,000 to A$160,000 depending on engine and option selection

Popular brand names available in the Australian market include: Boston Whaler, Trophy, Barcrusher, Baja, and Quintrex.

HIGH PERFORMANCE BOATS

SCARAB
This photo is used with permission from: Steve Gow Marine

Types of boats

Sometimes referred to as 'Miami-Vice boats' popular from the 1980's TV series. High performance boats are the sleek sports cars of the recreational boating world, offering high speeds and precise handling to boaters who prefer their thrills full throttle. Marrying big horsepower with sleek hulls results in boats that are equally at home slicing through ocean swells or tearing up inland lakes. Cranking offshore or simply relaxing in a cove, performance boats deliver lots of smiles per hour.

Technical Information

Hull Construction -	Fibreglass
Minimum Length -	19 feet (5.79m)
Maximum Length -	50 feet (15.24m)
Maximum Capacity -	8 people
Trailerable -	Yes but only to about 26 feet (7.92m)
Propulsion Type -	Outboard engine, Shaftdrive engine, Sterndrive engine, jet engine
Sleeping -	Yes, very basic in some makes, effectively for 2 people camping style.
Price Guide (brand new) -	A$80,000 to A$200,000 depending on engine and option selection

Popular brand names available in the Australian market include: Fastlane, Cigarette, and Kaos.

Types of boats

INBOARD SKI/WAKEBOARD BOATS

MB BOAT
This photo is used with permission from: MB Boats Australia

Types of boats

lInboard propulsion delivers the power to tow skiers and boarders and allow for the necessary speed to create tricks, and jumps. However, while wakeboard and ski boats look similar, skiers and boarders have opposing goals.

Wake-boarders want a giant wake to launch from as they cross from left to right behind the boat. Featuring V-drive engines set close to the transom and wide, deep hulls; inboard wakeboard boats carve the steep, large wakes that riders love.

Water-skiers want acceleration, and as little wake as possible. Underneath the water, the shape of the hull and the configuration and placement of the engine, propeller and drive shaft cause inboard ski boats to throw a slight wake that is easy for a skier to cross. They accelerate rapidly to "pop" skiers from the water and turn crisply.

Technical Information

Hull Construction -	Fibreglass
Minimum Length -	16 feet (4.87m)
Maximum Length -	28 feet (8.53m)
Maximum Capacity -	8 people
Trailerable -	Yes
Propulsion Type -	Inboard Engine, V-Drive, Outboard and Sterndrive Engine
Sleeping -	No
Price Guide (brand new) -	A$50,000 to A$150,000 depending on engine and option selection

Popular brand names available in the Australian market include: Malibu, Nautique, MB, Streaker Boats, Tige, and Mastercraft

Types of boats

JET BOATS

JET BOAT
This photo is used with permission from: Streaker Boats

Types of boats

Most jet boats look and perform like Bow-Riders with spacious seating in front and back and a swim platform. Builders promote a propulsion system almost completely enclosed inside the hull, reducing the risk of damage from impact with obstacles or the bottom. They are fast, manoeuverable, offering an exciting ride and a fun tubing and/or boarding platform.

Technical Information

Hull Construction -	Fibreglass, Hypalon and PVC
Minimum Length -	14 feet (4.26m)
Maximum Length -	25 feet (7.62m)
Maximum Capacity -	10 people
Trailerable -	Yes
Propulsion Type -	Jet Engine
Sleeping -	No
Price Guide (brand new) -	A$35,000 to A$70,000 depending on engine and option selection

Popular brand names available in the Australian market include: Streaker Boats and Sea Doo.

WALKAROUNDS

TROPHY WALKAROUND
This photo is used with permission from: St Kilda Boat Sales

Types of boats

These may be the ultimate family fishers and are most popular in coastal waters, large bays and the Great Lakes where anglers pursue salmon or offshore ocean species. They are equipped with rod holders, live-wells and steps to the forward deck to make it easy to follow a big fish around the boat. Walkarounds feature stowaway family seating, a cosy Cuddy Cabin and Half Cabin with plumbing for a toilet and sink that make them a winner for saltwater and freshwater fishing, cruising, swimming and tubing or skiing.

Technical Information

Hull Construction -	Fibreglass and Aluminium
Minimum Length -	18 feet (5.48m)
Maximum Length -	28 feet (8.53m)
Maximum Capacity -	7 people
Trailerable -	Yes
Propulsion Type -	Outboard and Sterndrive Engine
Sleeping -	Yes, very basic in some makes, effectively for 2 people camping style.
Price Guide (brand new) -	A$40,000 to A$100,000 depending on engine and option selection

Popular brand names available in the Australian market include: Caribbean, Boston Whaler, Trophy, Baja, Barcrusher and Quintrex.

SPORTS CRUISERS

SEA RAY 275
This photo is used with permission from: St Kilda Boat Sales

Types of boats

These popular boats have all the comforts expected from recreational cruising boats, including a galley (kitchen), head (toilet) and at least one berth (sleeping quarters). Available amenities include; TV, heating, air conditioning, water heaters, electric anchors, power generators, and shore power systems.

Sterndrive models usually range in size from 20 feet to 35 feet (6.09m to 10.66m) making them most popular in saltwater and inland waterways.

Shaftdrive cruisers tend to be 35 to 100-feet long (10.66m to 30.38m) and have even more room for creature comforts. They feature a simpler drive mechanism that is often considered easier to maintain in saltwater. They are steered with a rudder, rather than by turning a propeller drive mechanism and sometimes require more skill to manage.

Due to the single level design and layout, quite often they have smaller cockpit areas and therefore can sometimes be difficult to socially fish or dive from. In most cases they have built-in lounges and entertaining areas that offer very little open or free space.

Technical Information

Hull Construction -	Fibreglass
Minimum Length -	20 feet (6.09m)
Maximum Length -	100 feet (30.48m)
Maximum Capacity -	50 people
Trailerable -	Some but usually only up-to about 24ft (7.31m)
Sleeping -	2-6 people in comfort. Usually V-Berth and Transverse Double
Propulsion Type -	Sterndrive engine, Shaftdrive engine
Price Guide (brand new) -	A$70,000 to A$1,000,000 depending on engine and option selection.

Popular brand names available in the Australian market include: Riviera, Maritimo, Bayliner, Sea Ray, Sunrunner and Four Winns.

Types of boats

FLYBRIDGE CRUISERS

CARRIBEAN 47
This photo is used with permission from: St Kilda Boat Sales

Types of boats

A *flying bridge* is a (usually open) area on top of, or at the side of, a ship's pilothouse, or closed bridge, that serves as an operating station for the ship's officers in good weather or when manoeuvering in port where good views along the ship sides are important. It is also a raised, usually second-story cockpit on a smaller boat, such as a sport-fisher.

These are very popular and classic looking boats with a pedigree going back to the 1960s from Florida in the USA. These are really popular here in Australia and offer tremendous value for money if you're looking for a classic style, deep V cruiser with terrific sea-handling capability, with huge open-spaced cockpits which is at the back-end of the boat.

Flybridge Cruisers have all the comforts expected from recreational cruising boats, including a galley (kitchen), head (toilet) and at least one berth (sleeping quarters). Available amenities include heating, air conditioning, water heaters electric anchors, power generators, and shore power systems.

Sterndrive models usually range in size from 24 feet (7.32m) to 27 feet (8.23m) making them ideal as entry-level cruisers, still trailerable and perfect for buyers who want to upgrade from a smaller trailerable boat. These are most popular in saltwater and are often seen moored off the coastline on swing-moorings (read later chapter: Where will you keep it).

Available with the unique dual helm-station design (Flybridge and Lower) these are ideal for owners who want to be protected from the elements, therefore, commanding the vessel from the lower station. However, when weather permits the visibility and fun from driving the vessel from the upper station (Flybridge) is really popular amongst boat owners. Either way, the benefit of a dual helm-station vessel is the choice of two driving positions.

Shaftdrive cruisers tend to be 28 to 70-feet long (8.53m to 21.33m) and have even more room for creature comforts. They feature a simpler drive mechanism that is often considered easier to maintain in saltwater. They are steered with a rudder, rather than by a turning propeller drive mechanism and sometimes require more skill to manage. In the larger style Flybridge models, the dual helm-station offering is not always available, so you will drive the boat from upstairs in the Flybridge.

The dual-level design layout with a large cockpit area and deep-V hull, makes a Flybridge perfect for open (blue) water cruising. This is ideal for social, game or tournament fishing and diving or simply as open space for entertaining.

Technical Information

Hull Construction -	Fibreglass
Minimum Length -	24 feet (7.31m)
Maximum Length -	70 feet (21.33m)
Maximum Capacity -	25 people
Cruising Speed -	20 knots
Top Speed -	30 knots
Trailerable -	Yes, but usually only up-to about 27ft (8.23m)
Sleeping -	Yes 2-8 people in comfort. Master double and guest room bunks.
Propulsion Type -	Sterndrive engine or Shaftdrive engine
Price Guide (brand new) -	A$120,000 to A$1,600,000 depending on engine and option selection

Popular brand names available in the Australian market include: Caribbean, Riviera and Maritimo.

Types of boats

TRAWLERS (Displacements or Semi-Displacement)

MAINSHIP 34
This photo is used with permission from: St Kilda Boat Sales

Types of boats

You might say Trawlers are designed for sailors who don't want to manage sails and halyards. The hulls are designed to move efficiently through the water with minimum horsepower and fuel consumption, which makes them ideal for long range cruising. Facilities for sleeping, cooking and plumbing make them ideal for weekends on the water with family and friends. These boats are also known as semi-displacement or displacement due to their hull design and shape.

Whilst not known for their speed through the water because they are not a planing hull, however their fuel economy is truly outstanding and it is said that the "journey is the reward".

Technical Information

Hull Construction -	Fibreglass and Aluminium
Minimum Length -	26 feet (7.92m)
Maximum Length -	80 feet (24.38m)
Maximum Capacity -	varies
Cruising Speed -	9 knots
Top Speed -	13 knots
Trailerable -	No
Propulsion Type -	Shaftdrive Engine
Sleeping -	Yes 2-8 people in comfort. Master double and guest room bunks.
Price Guide (brand new) -	A$400,000 to A$800,000 depending on engine and option selection

Popular brand names available in the Australian market include: Mainship, Grand Banks and Choy Lee.

HOUSEBOATS

HOUSEBOAT
This photo is used with permission from: Wayne Adolphson

Types of boats

Buying a houseboat is a great way to bring friends and family together. Designed to offer lake-house living on the water complete with spacious floor plans and modern amenities for entertaining, dining and sleeping. Houseboats are made for relaxing cruises, weekend getaways to boating destinations, and unlimited family boating fun. Houseboats are best suited for rivers, lakes, weirs, and coastal waterways. Great for boaters of all ages, houseboats are built in a wide selection of sizes and styles and can be customized to personal tastes.

Technical Information

Hull Construction -	Fibreglass and Aluminium
Minimum Length -	25 feet (7.62m)
Maximum Length -	100 feet (30.48m)
Maximum Capacity -	varies
Trailerable -	No
Sleeping -	Yes 4-14 people in comfort. Master double and guest room bunks.
Propulsion Type -	Outboard engine or Sterndrive engine.
Price Guide (brand new) -	A$100,000 to A$1,000,000 depending on engine and option selection

Popular brand names available in the Australian market include: Baldwin and Gibson.

Types of boats

MULTI-HULL POWER BOATS

POWERCAT
This photo is used with permission from: St Kilda Boat Sales

Types of boats

Catamarans are the most common style of multi-hull powerboat, and are often considered as an alternative to centre console boats. A pair of pontoon-like deep v-hulls delivers a softer ride than V-bottom boats; twin engines offer speed and power to head offshore. The large beam, i.e. width of boat, offers stability at rest, an excellent feature when carrying large crews. Speed, manoeuverability, and space on-board are the main factors for choosing multihull design in powerboats.

Models designed for fishing are extremely popular with both fresh and saltwater anglers, while catamarans outfitted with recreational and cruising amenities make excellent all-around boats, perfect for families who enjoy a variety of on-the-water activities. Also suitable as a dive boat they boast huge open cockpits, ideal for fishing or dive gear storage. It's their unique twin hull design that makes them a very sturdy platform for rough water.

A wide, airy main cabin is the trademark of catamaran cruisers along with lots of deck space for sunning. Fuel-efficient, they are ideal for long-range cruising and island hopping.

Technical Information

Hull Construction -	Fibreglass and Aluminium
Minimum Length -	16 feet (4.87m)
Maximum Length -	50 feet (15.24m)
Maximum Capacity -	8 people
Trailerable -	Yes, but only up to 26 feet (7.92m)
Propulsion Type -	Outboard engine, Sterndrive engine
Sleeping -	Yes 2-8 people in comfort. Master double and guest room bunks.
Price Guide (brand new) -	A$150,000 to A$400,000 depending on engine and option selection

Popular brand names available in the Australian market include: PowerCat, Noosa Cat, Cougar Cat, and Grady White.

Types of boats

'COOLEST' Boats in the world

I often get asked by curious boat owners; what do I think are the coolest power boats in the world? To this *my answer is* **Wally**.

Cool is an understatement that was highlighted in an earlier episode of Top Gear in the UK, with a race between a Wally and a Supercar. It was also a Wally that featured in the closing scenes of the motion picture Swordfish boasting an all-star cast including: John Travolta, Hugh Jackman and Halle Berry! Not forgetting the movie The Island, this also extensively featured a Wally as a boat of the future.

WALLY RANGE
This photo is used with permission from: Wally

82   Honey, let's buy a BOAT!

Types of boats

Wally Ethos

The international headquarters for Wally is in Monaco. Wally was born of a passion for performance, a passion for design and a passion for the sea. Every Wally expresses these three passions in every detail. From chic and sporty motorboats through legendary racer-cruisers to magnificent 'blue-ocean' sailing yachts, nothing else looks or performs like a Wally.

This passion driven approach has created a community in which top-flight sailors, owners and the Wally team come together to continually push the boundaries of marine enjoyment, creating a peerless customer experience in which taking delivery is just the beginning.

Wally Founder

Luca Bassani Antivari, Founder and President of Wally has been sailing for 40 years. Since the first custom-built yacht which he designed for his own family in 1991 he has been changing the industry.

He founded Wally in 1994 to satisfy the needs of other experienced and dissatisfied yachtsmen.

Under Luca's guidance Wally continues to innovate and is today the only two-time winner of the world's most important prize for industrial design, the Compasso d'Oro.

Wally Build

The shipyards are where Wally's passion takes form; where the complex and often ground breaking designs go from the drawing board and CAD screen to being a tangible reality. Wally has more than two decades of experience building the world's most innovative yachts and powerboats. They have pioneered the use of carbon fibre along the way and introduced numerous game changing innovations. Naturally only the best materials are used, coming together in a high-tech environment at the hands of the industry's foremost craftsmen.

Wally Power

WallyPower means a global design icon. The same DNA informs every model, from the classic WallyOne Day cruiser to the fastest yacht in the world, the Wally 118, which encompasses a revolutionary vertical bow and hull engineering that ensures unmatched stability and control. Intelligent ergonomic design and the finest materials complete the package with living spaces that are comfortable, stylish and contemporary.

The Wally Power range:
- WallyOne
- Wally 47
- Wally 55
- Wally 73
- WallyAce
- Wally 118

WallyOne

The WallyOne is the ultimate day boat. Its light, but strong composite hull is powered by two Yanmar engines delivering more than 630 hp, and the single-level deck is the perfect platform for relaxing, water sports, diving expeditions or transporting guests and supplies from ship to shore. The slender vertical forefoot, deep bulwarks and flared bow deliver a smooth ride even in the choppiest seas, and the topsides have been carefully shaped to maximize carrying capacity without sacrificing the narrow waterline beam needed for agile handling.

The beauty of the versatile WallyOne lies not only in its elegant lines, but also in its sophisticated performance and ease of use.

Types of boats

WALLYONE
This photo is used with permission from: Wally

Technical Information

Hull Construction -   Fibreglass, Titanium and Carbon Fibre
Maximum Length -   43 feet (13.12m)
Trailerable -   No
Propulsion Type -   Twin Yanmar Diesel Sterndrives 315hp each or twin 370hp option
Sleeping -   2 persons
Price Guide (brand new) - A$850,000 to A$1,100,000 depending on engine and option selection

Types of boats

Wally 47

The Wally 47 is a spacious sports cruiser that blends practicality with indulgence. Controlled by a simple joystick for ease of docking at low speed, or the more conventional wheel for handling at speeds of over 35 knots, the Wally 47 cuts through the sea with ease. Teak decks and carbon fibre components combine to create a chic design true to Wally's values of simplicity and performance. The interior of the Wally 47 can be specified either as a two-berth cruiser or as a large lounge and galley area for those looking for an amazingly spacious day boat.

WALLY 47
This photo is used with permission from: Darren Finkelstein

Technical Information

Hull Construction -	Fibreglass, Titanium and Carbon Fibre
Maximum Length -	48.2 feet (14.70m)
Trailerable -	No
Propulsion Type -	Twin Volvo Penta IPS600 Diesel (D6) 435hp each
Sleeping -	2 people + 1
Price Guide (brand new) -	A$1,500,000 to A$2,000,000 depending on engine and option selection

WALLY 55
This photo is used with permission from: Darren Finkelstein

For more information and terrific pictures visit: www.wally.com

4

Engines

Power to move

Boat Engines

Choosing the right type of engine for your boat is a very important matter. Depending on whether you're buying a new or used boat you may not actually have a choice; therefore it pays to understand what's under the hood, so to speak.

Weight and horsepower (hp) output will both have an impact on the performance and safety of your boat. If your boat is underpowered, its engine will be overworked causing poor fuel economy and will cause poor performance overall as a result. Additionally, if your boat is overpowered, it may be difficult to handle and exceed the safe operating speed it was designed for, therefore voiding warranty and your insurance in the process (more about that later).

Engines

Here are the different types of propulsion systems (engines) powering most boats in today's marketplace:

- Outboard Motors – two-stroke or four-stroke
- Inboard - also known as Shaftdrive
- Jet Boat
- Sterndrive - also known as Inboard/Outboard
- POD Drive
- V-Drive

The Single vs. Twin Engine Debate

Depending on the length of the boat and the philosophy of the boat builder, you may not usually get a choice of whether to have single or twin engines on your selected boat. It will be how the actual boat is built determining whether it will or can be fitted with a single engine or have twin engines.

Below is a comparison of the engine configurations between single and twin engines:

Single Engine

- Less maintenance
- Less fuel consumption
- Lighter to tow
- Smaller in size
- Harder to manoeuvre in a tighter space
- Less balance in the water
- More susceptible to side-ways rocking and rolling
- Less stable at rest

Twin Engines

- Easy to drive

    o With one engine forward and one engine in reverse she will spin within your own length.

    o More control

- Safer - if one engine doesn't work, the other still does and can get you home
- More maintenance, usually double the cost.
- More fuel consumption, but not twice as much.

    o Both engines don't have to work as hard.

- Easier to manoeuvre in tight spaces.
- Skipper has total control over boat.
- Better balance and stability at rest.

    o Using my counter balance theory, just like a see-saw

    o Another 300kg in the back of the boat to steady the side-ways rock and roll.

We fit most boats we sell to Tasmania boaties with twin engines because the main boating is offshore in open oceans. So having a spare engine makes good sense!

Engines

TIP: Most of the larger boats from say 30ft or longer (or Caribbean 26ft) will be a twin engine set up, so don't stress. If you're going offshore, out of the bay and into the blue open-water, it's best to have twin engines for the reliability and redundancy factor. Otherwise fit an auxiliary outboard engine (5hp to 25hp) to the stern (back) of your boat. That way you at least have a spare engine to motor you home in the event of a mechanical breakdown.

We fit most boats we sell to tasmanian boaties with twin engines because the main boating is offshore in open oceans. So having a spare engine makes good sense!

Size Does Matter

If you are able to choose the appropriate engine for your boat, then you must consider the size and weight of the boat, remember weight includes your passengers, a full tank of fuel, water and gear.

A good rule of thumb is to be as close as possible, to the maximum horsepower that your boat is rated for. Every new boat sold in Australia after 2006 is required to have an Australian Builders Plate (ABP) affixed to the hull in a visible spot. The ABP will formally advise you of the maximum weight and engine horsepower rating, that the boat builder recommends for the specific vessel.

Do not exceed the details published on your ABP, as your boat will be deemed unsafe; your insurance will be void and you and your passengers can be at risk. Further information on the ABP can be found later in the book.

Both weight and horsepower will have an impact on the performance of your boat. If your vessel is underpowered, your engine will work harder than it needs, possibly leading to more routine maintenance also, the boat will not perform to your expectations which may leave you unsatisfied with the boat. This may also account for higher fuel consumption.

Additionally, if your vessel is overpowered, it may exceed the safe operating speed that was designed for the vessel. Manufacturers and dealers will all have a recommended power package for each and every boat they manufacture and sell, so it pays to listen to their advice.

Pick Your Power

When looking at petrol engines (outboard or inboard), there are three distinct types of fuel delivery systems on the market. They are: Direct Fuel Injection (DFI), Electronic Fuel Injection (EFI) and the ageing Carburetor Fuel Systems.

Each fuel delivery system is unique in its own way and there are benefits to each system:

Direct-Fuel-Injection (DFI)

In a Direct Fuel Injection System, the fuel is directly injected into the engine's cylinders. This helps control and raise fuel economy and compression ratios in relation to the engine's overall performance. High and low pressure fuel pumps and fuel injectors are a couple of the key components when looking at the system.

Benefits

- Low emissions.
- Excellent fuel economy.
- Instant turn-key starting.

- Smooth idling.
- Reduced vapor lock in warmer climates.
- Ability to automatically adjust to altitude, air and water temperatures.
- Superior throttle response and power.
- Availability of self-diagnosis systems.
- Sealed fuel system (helps to eliminate fuel oxidation).

Electronic Fuel Injection (EFI)

Electronic Fuel Injection functions on three basic systems: fuel delivery system, air induction system, and the electronic control system.

The fuel delivery system maintains a constant pressure through the use of an electronic fuel pump. The air delivery system controls the amount of air needed to burn the fuel efficiently. Finally, the electronic control system or sometimes called the ECU unit controls the fuel injectors and determines how much fuel and air needs to be delivered into cylinders at any given time.

Benefits
- Uniform air and fuel distribution.
- Superior throttle response and power.
- Usually excellent fuel economy.
- Cold engine start ability.
- Availability of self-diagnosing systems.
- Low emissions (especially four-stroke).

Carbureted Fuel Systems

Carbureted engines have been around for several decades now. When looking at a carbureted engine, you will notice the carburetor on top of the engine. The carburetor controls the amount of air flow and fuel into the engine. This is a mechanical process controlled by a throttle body cable usually hooked to the throttle at the helm. Again, this is an all mechanical process.

Benefits

- Simple by design.
- Lowest initial cost.
- Higher emissions than EFI or DFI system.
- Poor fuel economy when compared to an EFI or DFI system.

Exercise Caution

An ageing carburetor engine has had a very poor reputation for reliability and maybe a potential fire danger.

Furthermore, in recent times, Club Marine, Australia's largest pleasure craft insurer, has seen a marked increase in the number of incidents of fires on petrol-fuelled craft, most notably inboard-powered ski boats. The fires generally begin in or around the engine and are almost universally caused by leaking fuel and the resultant build-up of explosive petrol vapours. Overwhelmingly, the incidents are linked to older craft, typically boats with ageing automotive engines usually modified or otherwise tinkered with by the owners or non-authorised technicians over the years. The cumulative effect of their efforts can have disastrous outcomes, as we've recently seen in the media. Petrol-fuelled boat engines have very specific requirements when it comes to fuel systems and safety procedures. They need to be regularly maintained and inspected by experienced marine technicians, who know where the trouble spots are and how to deal with them.

"Boats with car engines that have been converted, or marinised, are certainly over-represented when it comes to fires and explosions, and older boats are more prone to problems," said Club Marine's National Claims Manager, Phil Johnson. "Some conversions may not have been performed as professionally as owners might think and fuel leaks and electrical problems, such as non-spark-arrested starter motors or alternators, can turn some of these craft into floating time bombs."

Of particular concern to Club Marine are craft that are used primarily on a seasonal basis and that spend long periods of time inactive or in storage. Minor fuel leaks, and subsequent vapour pockets in bilges and other hard-to-detect areas, can result in catastrophic fires, damage and serious injury to occupants.

"That's why we have a special Inboard and Performance Ski-Boat assessment report that we require to be filled out in certain circumstances before providing insurance coverage for these craft," said Johnson.

"Many boat owners don't realise that fuel vapour can build up undetected on their boats over time."

"Something as simple as a minor fuel spill when refuelling can produce a pocket of vapour in a boat. Then, all it takes is a spark or naked flame and in a split second the boat is engulfed in flames. "In our experience, boats with dedicated inboard marine engines tend to have less claims for fire-related damage than those with converted car engines," said Johnson.

TIP: To remove any doubt whatsoever, if you're considering buying an older style boat with petrol carburetor based engines, then please arrange a formal pre-purchase inspection of all marine craft that are powered by a petrol carburetor engine, as part of your purchase criteria. The safety of you and your guests is your responsibility.

Outboard Engines

The definition of an outboard motor is a detachable engine mounted onto outboard brackets on the stern of your boat. Today's outboard motors range in horsepower from 1.0 hp to over 350 hp per engine. Outboard motors can be used in all types of waters. There are two general types of outboard motors: two-stroke and four-stroke motors.

Outboard – Two-Stroke

OUTBOARD
This photo is used with permission from Mercury Marine

Two-stroke Benefits

- Generally better acceleration out of the hole (from a stationary start) and at top-end.
- Overall excellent power to weight ratio.
- Basic models are simple by design.
- Generally lower priced than a four-stroke (carbureted two-stroke only).
- No need to change the oil.
- Generally weighs less than a four-stroke.
- Usually better fuel efficiency than carbureted two-strokes (comparable to four-stroke).
- Usually quieter than carbureted two-stroke (comparable to four-stroke).

Additional Benefits for Two-stroke DFI

- DFI versions have lower emissions than carbureted two-stroke that meet all state standards (comparable to four-stroke).
- Much better fuel efficiency than carbureted two-strokes (comparable to four-stroke).
- Much quieter than carbureted two-stroke (comparable to four-stroke).
- Engine Management Systems.
- Electronic Ignition Systems.

Engine Brands

Brands for Outboard Motor – Two-strokes:
- Evinrude - E-tec
- Mercury - OptiMax

Engines

Outboard – Four-Stroke

OUTOBARD
This photo is used with permission from Mercury Marine

One noticeable difference between two-stroke and four-stroke engines is the weight of the similar horse-powered engines. Four-strokes tend to be heavier than a two-stroke engine of comparable horsepower. Two-stroke engines use a petrol and oil mixture, while a four-stroke burns petrol. A four-stroke engine is more like a car engine including an oil filter and generally has lower torque than two-strokes.

Four-Stroke Benefits

- Low emissions – Meets all state standards, including the 5 star rating in Australia.
- Strong top-end and good acceleration.
- Excellent fuel economy.
- Quiet operation.
- Engine management systems.
- Electronic ignition systems.
- The oil is added to the engine rather than the fuel, allowing for clean and efficient fuel consumption.

Engines

Engine Brands

Brands for Outboard Motor – four-strokes:
- Honda
- Mercury – Verado Supercharged
- Suzuki
- Yamaha

Inboard Shaftdrive - (Diesel)

DIESEL SHAFT
This photo is used with permission from Richard Spooner, John Barbar & SeKilsa Boat Sales

DIESEL SHAFT
This photo is used with permission from Richard Spooner, John Barbar & SeKilsa Boat Sales

Diesel engines rely on compression to power the engine. Compared to a traditional petrol engine, the engines are similar by design, as they have crankshafts, cylinders and pistons; however, the fuel systems are completely different and more complex on a diesel engine.

Diesel engines range in size and horsepower. Diesel engines are widely used in other parts of the world. Whilst they are typically found in boats larger than 35 feet, the Bertram / Caribbean 28 is a highly successful exception. The main reason diesel engines are not commonly used in smaller boats is cost. The engine in general weighs and costs a lot more than a petrol engine, sometimes expect to pay double the price. However, they are used in larger vessels because of their ability to produce torque, safety and better fuel economy.

In general, diesel engines run at lower RPM's than traditional petrol engines.

Benefits

- No carbon monoxide to worry about in cabins or on the back of boats.
- Excellent torque.
- Long life expectancy.
- Low running costs.
- Majority of the engines weigh more than a traditional petrol engine.
- Non-explosive fuel.

Engine Brands

Brands for Diesel Inboard Engines:
- CAT
- Cummins
- Mercruiser
- Yanmar
- Volvo

Engines

Inboard Shaftdrive - (Petrol)

PETROL SHAFT
This photo is used with permission from
St Kilda Boat Sales

PETROL SHAFT
This photo is used with permission from
St Kilda Boat Sales

While similar to what is under the hood of your car, petrol engines used in marine applications are modified to make them marine engines. Petrol inboard engines (or called Gasoline in the USA) range in horsepower from 90 hp to over 1000 hp per engine and are used in a variety of engines from tow sport boats to large cruisers.

In an inboard engine configuration, the engine sits amidships, with a drive running through the bottom of the boat to a propeller, with a separate rudder used for steering. A transmission is often used to transfer power from the engine to the propeller. Exhaust is passed through the stern of the boat. Inboards are also common for tow sports such as water-skiing and wakeboarding as they allow the propeller to be brought forward off the back of the boat, providing area for platforms to assist skiers in entering and exiting the boat.

Benefits:
- Simple drive system can lower maintenance.
- No means to trim propeller.
- Low running costs.

- Quiet and out of the way.

Engine Brands

Brands for Petrol Inboard Engines:

- Mercruiser
- Volvo Penta

Jet Engine / Propulsion

Jet
This photo is used with permission from Mercury Marine

These propulsion systems have the advantage of having no propeller to cause potential danger to people in the water and marine life. They are usually inboard engines that take in water that flows through a pump powered by an impeller. The water is then discharged at high pressure through a nozzle that propels the boat forward. The nozzle swivels to provide steering to the boat. Most personal watercraft use jet drives.

Engines

TIP: When power is not being applied, a jet driven vessel loses its steering because it is the stream of water that steers the boat. Keep hands, feet and hair away from the pump intake and do not operate in shallow water.

Engine Brands

Brands for Jet Boat Engine and Propulsion:
- Mercruiser
- Yanmar
- Rotax
- Kawasaki

Sterndrives – also known as Inboard / Outboard

STERNDRIVE
This photo is used with permission from Mercury Marine

STERNDRIVE
This photo is used with permission from Mercury Marine

104 Honey, let's buy a BOAT!

Engines

A Sterndrive consists of an engine and drive connected to one another through the transom of a boat. A Sterndrive is sometimes called an Inboard/Outboard (I/O), reflecting its design. It is designed so that its engine is inside and enclosed by the boat, while the propulsion system (out drive) is outside of the boat and in the water. Sterndrives are available in both petrol and diesel configurations.

The out drive can be trimmed - moved up or down - and has a propeller attached to the end of it to propel the boat forward and reverse. This is also the main steering system for the boat as it can turn side to side. Because the engine is in the boat, rather than being supported by the transom as in an outboard, larger engines with greater horsepower can be used.

Sterndrive engines can come in a variety of different functions depending on their intended use; drives are available with one or two propellers on a single Sterndrive. They can also be used in tandem with two drives on a single boat, each with single or multiple propellers.

Like most things and similar to the motor vehicle industry, the diesel version will be a lot more expensive than the petrol, sometimes double the cost. So do your sums to see it you can actually save more than what the extra cost is for having diesel engine. Typically as recreational boaters, you may never be able to justify the price difference in fuel savings over the lifetime of your boat.

Benefits

- Allows for ease of control and steering in forward or reverse.
- Can be used on petrol or diesel engine packages.
- Relatively low maintenance.
- Quiet and efficient.
- Good value.

Engine Brands

Brands for Sterndrive Engines:
- Mercruiser
- Volvo Penta

Pod Drive

PODS
This photo is used with permission from Volvo Penta

PODS
This photo is used with permission from Volvo Penta

With ongoing technological advancement the innovative use of joystick-control systems is the perfect remedy for boat manoeuvring and docking woes. Pod drives and legs allow you to dock in a safe and relaxed way, regardless of close quarters, cross currents or side winds. The intuitive and natural user interface gives you total boat control with one hand, meaning anybody can dock safely with total confidence. Pods are available in both petrol and diesel configurations.

Pod systems also deliver innovative navigation features such as Mercruiser's "Skyhook", an electronic anchor that holds your boat in place based on GPS positioning, regardless of wind and water conditions. Waypoint control allows you to set a course on your chart plotter that your boat will follow automatically. With pod drives, boat control and navigation have never been easier or more precise. The future of boating is here for everyone to enjoy.

The MerCruiser Axius system uses a joystick to control steering, throttles and shifters at the same time, also offering complete boat manoeuverability with one hand. The interface is simple and intuitive: move the joystick in the direction you want to go, and the further you move it, the faster the boat will travel in that direction. With the Axius System your Sterndrives move independently of each other, allowing them to achieve the lateral movement needed to pull off close-quarter manoeuvres with ease.

Volvo Penta IPS is the modern inboard system, superior to inboard shafts in every vital aspect – handling, on-board comfort and performance. Those benefits have made Volvo Penta IPS the by far most popular pod system for leisure boats.

The joystick is perhaps the most well-known feature of Volvo Penta IPS, making it possible to dock in a new and completely intuitive way. Since its release it has been accompanied by many other smart features, such as Dynamic Positioning System and Sportfish mode. The latest generation of Volvo Penta controls has integrated buttons for Low-speed mode, Single-lever mode and Cruise control, making it even easier to enjoy boating with Volvo Penta IPS.

The range consists of ten models, from IPS350 to IPS1200, matched to three different pod sizes and available for twin, triple and quadruple installations. This makes Volvo Penta IPS suitable for yachts from 30 to 100 feet.

Now also for semi-planing craft Joystick docking, minimal noise and vibrations, virtually no smoke or smell. These highly appreciated benefits are now also available for trawlers and other semi-planing craft.

Benefits of Pods

- Joystick Functionality.
- Move sideways and at an angle.
- Rotate in own length or 360° on an axis.
- Intuitive, proportional control of thrust and speed in any direction.
- Enhanced docking control mode.
- Safety, reliability & durability.
- Shallow draft design for less water displacement.
- Precision navigation.
- GPS anchoring.
- Auto heading.
- Waypoint control.
- Comfortable fit.

The ergonomically designed joystick is built for comfort and ease of use, giving you better handling and more intuitive control.

Engine Brands

Brands of Pods drives:

- Mercruiser - Axius
- Volvo Penta - IPS
- Cummins - Zeus

V-Drive

V-DRIVE
This photo is used with permission from St Kilda Boat Sales

V-DRIVE
This photo is used with permission from St Kilda Boat Sales

The difference between a v-drive and direct-drive is the drive shaft itself. A V-drive is shaped like the letter V. The shaft goes from the motor to a transmission inside the boat and back toward the prop. A direct-drive has a straight shaft that goes from the engine out to the prop. A direct-drive engine is located mid-boat, whereas V-drive boats have engines in the rear.

Skiers like direct-drives because they have flat bottoms which create small wakes and handle well depending upon how the ballast tank of a ski boat is filled, a v-drive can manoeuvre a boat through the water, cutting the surface and creating a wake boarder or skier's dream wake.

Benefits
- Low speed manoeuvering capability.
- Skiers like direct-drives because they have flat bottoms which create small wakes and handle well.
- Some say cheaper to maintain.

Engine Brands

Brands of V Drive:
- PCM
- Mercruiser

5

Boat Trailers

Limitless Freedom

Boat Trailers

Boating offers many dimensions to the sense of freedom; you can tow a boat to different bodies of water all over the country (your choices are endless). This is just one of the many reasons boating is so popular. With a trailerable boat you're free to boat just about anywhere: lakes, rivers, bays or inlets. Trailering is a great way to explore different waterways in your state or region. Using a boat trailer is also the most affordable way to store a boat.

Important Boating Safety Tips:

Getting Started

If you've never trailered a boat, there are several things you need to consider. First is the towing capacity of your car, truck or SUV. You can find this information in your vehicle owner's manual. Generally, small family sedans are not suitable for towing. However a small, aluminium Tinnie may not present a problem provided you have appropriate towing equipment installed on your car.

A basic guide to vehicle towing capacity:
- Sedans e.g. Commodore or Falcons: up to 1,600kg
- 4x4 (medium size) e.g. X3, Q5, CRV, Murano, Pathfinder: up to 2,400kg
- 4x4 (large size) e.g. X5, Q7, Landcruiser, Prado, Discovery or Patrol: up to 3,500kg

Warning: Please consult your vehicle owner's manual for limitations and your local registration authority to find out what's applicable to your state or territory. Also consult your towbar supplier or fitter, to find the best match for your car and for your budget. Towbars, fittings and braking systems can be expensive.

TIP: Towing regulations are a state- or territory-based law. So if you're towing outside your state or territory border, then please check before you leave home as to the destination's towing requirements. The rules aren't the same for each state or territory and sadly ignorance is no excuse.

Look for Certified Trailers
Australian Design Rule (ADR) Compliance

No trailer is permitted on Australian roads unless it complies with the ADR. Trailers must be compliant in the areas of identification plates, capacity ratings, couplings, safety chains, lighting, winches, brakes, and registration.

Boat Trailers

Inspectors visit the manufacturer and physically inspect each boat trailer model for compliance to all certification standards. A manufacturer participating in this program must certify all models as fitted with all factory supplied equipment on a model year basis.

At the time of registration, your trailer will be physically inspected for compliance and the Vehicle Identification Number (VIN) is recorded by the registration authority. This is why an Australian manufactured trailer that is compliant is a safer and better choice of purchase.

TRAILER
This photo is used with permission from
St Kilda Boat Sales

Weight Considerations

In all states and territories of Australia, a vehicle can tow a trailer with a mass less than:
- The tow vehicle's towbar rating and
- The tow vehicle manufacturer's recommended maximum trailer mass.

If the manufacturer has not specified a recommended mass, the vehicle can tow a trailer up to the unloaded mass of the tow vehicle, provided the trailer has brakes. If the laden float is up to 2,000 kg, overrun (Breakaway) brakes will suffice. If the laden trailer is over 2,000 kg, the brakes must be independently operated — that is, electric or hydraulic together with an approved breakaway system.

All trailers exceeding 750 kg MUST have brakes fitted, which means it is illegal to tow a trailer above that weight that does not have suitable brakes.

Weighing In

Your boat owner's manual will list the "dry weight" of your boat. This is the weight of the boat, less fuel, water and gear. Now add the tow weight which is the actual weight of the trailer only, when not carrying a load, this is called the TARE. Make sure when you're assessing your vehicle's towing capacity that you add several hundred kg's to the dry weight of the boat to account for those extras. Be sure to do the exact calculation, don't guess!

Every litre of fuel and water equals 1 kg of weight, so by the time you add the weight of this and the kids' bikes and all the stuff you'll load into your boat to go on holidays, you are likely to be overweight. This is a very dangerous practice and will cause both your car and boat insurances to be void for towing overweight loads. If per chance you are involved in an accident or stopped by the police or authorities for inspection, you're likely to make a bad situation worse.

TIP: Maybe even take your fully laden car together with boat on the trailer to a public weigh bridge and for a few well-spent dollars, you'll get the exact weight; simple with no guessing!

Muscle Power

As the weight, length and width (beam) of a given boat increase, so does the muscle power needed to launch and retrieve it. A small boat may be easy for one person to handle at the ramp, but larger boats, generally those more than 25-feet, may require additional hands. Don't be afraid to ask for help at the ramp if you need it. Other trailer boaters are happy to help, so ask with a smile and be sure to tell them you're a beginner.

Consult Your State Laws

Trailering laws vary somewhat from state to state and often are based on weight and beam. Make sure to research before you buy your boat and ensure the research is also carried out when planning your trip with the boat.

Basic Trailering Checklist

Never tow your boat trailer before you check to be sure:
- Coupler, hitch and hitch ball are of the same size.
- Coupler and safety chains are safely secured to the hitch of tow vehicle.
- All fasteners are properly tightened.
- Boat is securely tied down to the trailer (winch line is not a tie down).
- Wheel lug nuts are properly tightened.
- Wheel bearings are properly adjusted and maintained.
- Load is within the maximum load carrying capacity.
- Tyres are properly inflated.
- All trailer lighting is working properly.

- Trailer brakes are properly adjusted and working (if trailer is so equipped).
- Local and state requirements regarding brakes and any additional equipment that may be required are met.

A Word on Wheels

The quality and condition of your trailer wheels are critical to the safety of you and others on the road. You should regularly inspect wheels for wear and bearings for proper lubrication. To make the latter an easier process, consider a product like Bearing Buddies, which keeps bearings lubricated. These systems also reduce how often you need to repack your bearings.

Adding a cap to your bearings will help contain the grease, preventing it from splattering on the hubs of your wheels. Carry a spare bearing kit as a precaution for problems during travel. Keeping bearings lubricated is important, so invest in a grease gun and some specialty marine grease.

Having a spare wheel and the tools to change a flat is a wise decision when towing a boat. Spare wheels can be secured to a trailer with special hardware. Carriers come in models for various tyre types and in different mounting options. Use a cover to protect the spare from the elements.

Security

Locks are one of the best methods to deter thieves from your boat and trailer. Trailer locks can be purchased for the coupler, spare tyre, as well as large models for the hub of your trailer wheels. Some insurance companies will not charge an excess if a theft has occurred whilst an 'approved trailer lock' was fitted.

For the boat, there are locks to secure outboard motors and propellers.

Motor units cover the transom mounting clamps. To secure your propeller, two options exist. One is a specialty lock that replaces the prop nut and washer, allowing the outboard engine to operate only when unlocked. The other option is a larger prop lock, which connects the propeller to the out drive, or lower unit. This style of lock must be removed for the motor to work.

Maintenance and Storage

To prevent your boat from rolling during storage, use wheel chocks, especially if on a slope. Units can be purchased in plastic or metal models to hold trailer tyres in place. Another handy item is a jack wheel stop. This flat, plastic ring encircles the jack's wheel, preventing it from moving.

Depending on the weight of your boat and the distance you need to move it, you may want to consider a trailer dolly. Dollies let you move your boat trailer by connecting at the trailer coupler. The dolly's long handle reduces your need to bend and lift the trailer, which greatly limits the potential for back strain. The unit's wheels also make moving a trailer an easy operation.

Another accessory that helps move your trailer is a jack which mounts to the trailer's tongue. Jacks often come with most, but not all, trailers when purchased. By cranking the jack's handle, you can raise or lower the front end of your trailer. The jack's wheel also facilitates moving the trailer when not being towed, as jacks come with a wheel to support the front of a trailer.

Boat Trailers

 **TIP:** Don't forget to use a few bricks or purpose-built wheel chocks to chock the tyres so the trailer won't move and the braking system (if fitted) can be left in the off position. Otherwise the salt-air can lock and corrode the brakes fast onto the wheel.

CAR, BOAT & TRAILER
This photo is used with permission from: StKilda Boat Sales

Lights and Wiring

For safe travel and to meet transportation laws, the lighting on your trailer must work at all times. Before towing, ensure all signal and brake lights are functioning. It's a good idea to carry spare bulbs if you need to replace one. If a light isn't working and you can't isolate the problem, a small accessory can be plugged into your vehicle's plug. If the unit's lights go green when signals and brakes are used, the automobile wiring works and the trailers wiring is the problem.

To replace wiring or lights you can buy parts individually or in a kit. Most kits include the necessary mounting hardware. Lighting fixtures come in a variety of models with different features, like submersible trailer lights, corrosion resistant materials and LED light sets for longer burning hours. You can also purchase reflectors for your trailer to replace broken ones or to simply increase the unit's visibility.

Toolkit

A toolkit or storage box that you can keep in your vehicle or boat for your trailer is a sound investment. Beyond standard tools (such as pliers, a ratchet set, screwdrivers, etc), the box should also contain trailer-specific items (bearing grease, electrical tape, scissors, tyre pressure gauge) and replacement parts (bearings, pins, light bulbs, etc).

Your trailer plays a critical role in your boating activity, by carrying your vessel to and from the water. The above accessories make towing and launching your boat an easier and safer process, so you can enjoy more time on the water and less time on the pavement fixing problems that could have been prevented.

Australian Compliance

All Australian vehicles must comply with all relevant Standards for Registration and must be roadworthy at all times for use on public roads.

Below is a listing of the responsible authorities in Australia:
- Australian Transport Safety Bureau
- Austroads
- Commonwealth Department of Transport & Regional Services
- Department of Infrastructure - Victoria
- Department of Transport - Tasmania
- Department of Transport and Works - Northern Territory
- Department of Transport - Western Australia
- Department of Urban Services - ACT
- Main Roads Western Australia
- Queensland Department of Main Roads
- Queensland Transport
- NSW Department of Transport
- Roads and Traffic Authority NSW
- Transport SA - Permits
- Transport SA - Registration & Licensing
- Vic Roads

Speed Restrictions

Since December 1998, all trailers can be towed at whatever speed is sign-posted for that specific road. However, some vehicle manufacturers have placed restrictions on the maximum recommended speed for their vehicle when towing heavy loads. You need to know if such a recom-

Boat Trailers

mendation exists, as your insurer could refuse to cover you if an accident happens as a result of exceeding the recommended speed, or you could be charged by the police for dangerous driving.

Even if you are legally entitled to travel faster, you need to remember that your boat will probably fare much better if you keep around 80 km/h.

Learner drivers are not permitted to drive a vehicle while it is towing a trailer.

6

Where will you keep it?

7 storage ideas for stress free boating

"How big is your garage?" asked the salesman, "how big does it need to be?" ... asked the eager boat buyer. Not everyone has the luxury of being able to build a garage to store the boat of your dreams. Given the varying sizes and high cost of real estate in suburbia, not every boat will fit into your garage and nor will some boat owners want it kept there. Your towing vehicle will usually determine a lot which we've talked about earlier. Some boats will just be way too big to tow, so storage options may be limited.

The choices for boat storage are fairly simple and depending on your storage location, can be difficult to arrange. Basically, your choices for storage are either on land (dry storage) or on water (wet storage), so let's explore this in detail.

Where will you keep it?

Land (Dry Storage)

Land storage is for trailerable boats and begins at your home. The very convenience and nature of home storage means it is the cheapest of all storage options available. Having a boat kept locked in your garage at home offers the security and peace of mind of always having her under your watchful eye. Security of your boat is of prime importance. A garage has a roof and walls, which serves well to protect it by keeping birds out and the boat free from bird poop which is one of the prime benefits of enclosed storage. The acid in bird droppings if left unattended will eat into your boat's covers leaving oil like stains. Please don't under estimate the importance of having a roof overhead. Also have you ever noticed that particularly in summer, we get that orange dirty rain? When dust and dirt particles are picked up over arid regions of Australia they are carried many miles and fall from the sky as muddy rain. So a roof overhead is really important, otherwise a decent full-length boat cover will suffice in lieu.

BOAT IN GARAGE
This photo is used with permission from: Jodi & Anthony Eden

What about wildlife making a home in your unattended boat. Did you know that possums are an endangered species? If you don't cover your boat, expect a family of possums to take up residency. Whilst to a possum, your uncovered boat will offer a safe haven and free accommodation for many years protected from the elements, there is a downside. The 'bloody possums' will crap everywhere, eat your seats and destroy your boat if left unattended. Depending where in Australia you live, the possums will be the least of your worries. For those who reside in Far North Queensland and around the tropics in WA and in Darwin, I've heard of owners having to put up with small crocs, death adders and brown snakes curled up inside their boats (now that will take the blood pressure to new levels!). This is why it's important to fully cover your boat to avoid surprises of all shapes and sizes. In addition to the wildlife you'll also need to consider cyclones and violent storms and whilst we can't prevent them, we certainly can prepare for natural disasters. Thunderstorms, cyclones and monsoons are three natural causes that wreak havoc on Australian marinas. During cyclone season, opt to store your boat in a warehouse or another enclosed storage space for safety. If you don't have storage space, be sure to tape-up all glass windows, strategically place sand bags, and put away items that may shift and fall during turbulent waters. Equip your boat with a proper bonding system that will guide lightening to the ground. It pays to talk to your local authorities and seek their recommendations for safe storage advice during these times.

Size is everything

Its human nature to exaggerate size and dimensions, so ensure you get the exact measurements of a boat on her trailer before you purchase, ideally get them in writing from the boat seller or measure it yourself for peace of mind. Make sure the measurement is taken with medium-air in the trailer tyres and that you get the ground to the very top measured. You may need to remove the boat covers for transport, so the measurements should be typically ground to the top of a windscreen, if it is fixed and non-removable. Most boat Dealers/Brokers will have that information readily available to answer buyer's questions. Be sure to ask private sellers to measure it for you. After-all if it doesn't fit in the garage, how can you realistically buy it?

As mentioned earlier, you want a lockable garage that is safe with a roof and four walls to keep all unwelcome guests out. The dimensions of your garage should be large enough to store your boat comfortably. One of my earliest memories was Dad going into the garage at home; today we call it his man-cave, usually after dinner and on weekends, to simply mess around with his tools and tidy-up. Boy was it the cleanest garage going round, but this was his place, his little hide-out, a getaway from the rigours of family life. I later grew to understand that this was "his-time" not because my sisters and I were too much too handle, but more importantly a chance for Dads to de-stress, have a beer (or three) and enjoy quiet time. In today's world, the importance of "me time" becomes really evident with the issues surrounding "men's-health" and much has been written about the role of a tool-shed, garage and/or workshop. The idea of boat storage in your garage at home is ideal for so many reasons. So if your boat fits and your vehicle can tow, then this should be considered as your first choice, if possible.

Ensure your driveway and street access is suitable for reversing your boat. Walk the length of the driveway and take a good look at the surface. Check the width of the roadway out front of the house, remember your vehicle and trailer will need a bit of space to either swing out when leaving home heading to the water, or to straighten the trailer up when beginning your reversing manoeuvre. A quiet side-street off the main road is simply perfect which means you'll have a little more breathing space rather than contending with the traffic flow and dealing with impatient drivers of other vehicles.

Where will you keep it?

> **TIP:** For those that are on a main road and will contend with traffic flow, don't stress. Ask your spouse to put on a high-visibility vest (usually about $20 from your local hardware) and have them be your spotter to walk with the front of your vehicle to appease the traffic. This will also serve as a great way for you both to participate as a team by working together.

Check your driveway surface; ideally an even surface with good drainage is preferred. Otherwise it is really hard for your vehicle to get good traction when in the wet. Slow reversal is the best way, ensuring a steady passage. Ask your spotter to walk behind your reversing vehicle to ensure that it's a clear path. Communicate loudly with each other through an open driver's window (or with walkie talkies). Turn the radio off and don't answer your mobile phone, you need to be focussed and don't let your mind wander.

Ensure that the width of your driveway entrance is suitable, check the gutter at the street is even and not with a dip. These dips tend to scratch your tow bar and the underside of the vehicle and the loud whack of the tow-bar hitting concrete are also off-putting. It's really important to remember the time when you're usually reversing your boat back up the driveway is usually after a long day spent on the water. You often feel tired, grumpy and sensitive, so be mindful.

Borrow a garage

If you don't have a garage at home to use, you may want to ask to borrow one. Sometimes you can get lucky by having someone offer you the

Where will you keep it?

use of their garage. Often one of your boating friends may have some unused area of an office, warehouse or factory space available. Even if it's a corner tucked away, so long as you can cover the boat and trailer with a tarpaulin or tonneau cover and it's secure, she'll be fine.

In the winter months when your boat won't be used as much it's really important to run the engine (either Sterndrive or Outboard) for a few minutes, at least every 2-3 weeks in the off season. To do this - buy a set of "earmuffs," an engine flushing attachment for your boat from any boating chandler or marine retailer. A set of earmuffs will cost about $15 and once connected to a standard garden hose with a click-on style connection will enable you to run your engine when not near a waterway (bay or lake); otherwise dry running your engine will cause damage. Regularly flush the engine and keep her nice and lubricated with fresh water thereby removing salt. If you're using your boat in fresh-water, there is no need to flush your engine.

TIP: When you flush your engine, first turn on the battery switch (if you have one) connect the garden hose and turn ON the tap water. Ensure that you have water running through the hose and connect the earmuffs to the engine leg ensuring the intake grills are covered properly. You will then have water running through the engine and you should see water coming out of the telltales or exhaust. Don't start-up the engine until you have seen water coming out. Once it's visible, keep the propeller clear (of people and hose) and turn the engine ON and let her run for a few minutes. Once finished, turn-engine OFF first, then turn OFF the hose and remove earmuffs. Job's done!

Use 240v electricity to run a small battery charger it is a great way to trickle charge to your battery in the off-season.

Self-Storage

Self-storage is quickly becoming a realistic and viable alternative should you not have the luxury of a garage at home to store your boat. A self-storage facility, offers space of differing sizes that is available for rental. With some self-storage facilities, you are able to rent a secure space for a minimum period of time, usually one month and beyond.

Spaces are mostly in very large warehouse style structures offering terrific trailer access with wonderfully smooth and even surfaces making towing and vehicle traction a breeze. Typically well secured 24 hours a day, self-storage is an effective way to store your boat and trailer.

Trailer Park

Trailer park storage is a viable alternative that is usually located at most marinas. This means easy water access to your preferred boating destination, one of the main benefits.

Trailer park storage is the same as permanently renting a car parking bay in a parking complex where you will keep the trailer and boat. When you want to go boating, you hook up the boat to your vehicle and launch and retrieve her yourself. By using the private and non-public boat ramp, you will avoid the car park and launch congestion.

Where will you keep it?

TRAILER PARK
This photo is used with permission from
St Kilda Marina

After you've been boating for the day, you can wash and clean your boat, de-junk her in readiness for your next day out. Simple to engine flush using your trusty earmuffs is essential to rid the engine of salt. Take time to relax, have a drink and care for your boat; she will appreciate your love and serve you well.

After talking to many boat owners, the disadvantages of trailer park storage are mainly centred on the boat being stored outdoors. The sun is harsh to the shiny fibreglass (gelcoat) surface of your hull. Boat covers struggle long-term as well and whilst quality Sunbrella brand of marine canvases are UV treated, the sun will eventually damage all covers after a few years. The solution will then be to replace your covers.

Where will you keep it?

TIP: The bloody seagulls are a problem as well. Keep them off your boat using Gull Sweep, rubber snakes and even fishing lines. Seagulls left unattended on your boat will spell disaster and most certainly a new set of covers, sooner rather than later. Ensure you use a pressure washer, to remove bird poo, as the acid will eat the cover and create tears.

Boat Clears (plastic looking covers that are see-thru) they are very fragile too. Always wash off the salt after going boating with a sponge, mild detergent and chamois dry. If you don't, the sun will bake the salt onto the clear and before you know it, your clear will appear all cloudy and tinged with brown. This is bad, very bad in fact, as your clears are now burnt because the sun has actually cooked the salt onto it. This cloudiness will spread; sadly there is nothing you can do to reverse this condition, other than replacement.

Good quality clears are made from a UV treated PVC like product called VYBAK which is not just simple plastic and imported from the USA. The really good clears are made with the crystal clear product called Strata Glass. PVC is a cheap alternative that tends to shrink, stretch and ripple when kept in the outdoors especially through a harsh Aussie summer. Ask your boat seller to identify what type of clears you have, so you can match or replace them as needed. Typically a good set of VYBAK clears with last about 4 years, if they are regularly washed and treated. There is a terrific cleaning product available called Plexus. Spay it on and it truly works wonders on the clears. Plexus is available through most boat chandlers and some hardware stores. Alternatively, wash your clears with soapy warm water on both sides, then wash down with water and wipe over with a chamois to dry.

Where will you keep it?

You may wish to request a trailer park spot away from the prevailing winds, meaning storing her where she will be protected. Try to keep her out of the direct sunlight and cover the boat with a tarpaulin or tonneau when not in use.

Yard or Dry Storage, (Hard Stand)

Congratulations, you've made one of the more difficult decisions with regard to boat storage, which is to pay a marina for storing your boat. For some boat owners it's a really hard decision to swallow paying out those high fees for boat storage, when space is sometimes available for free at home or work.

RACK
This photo is used with permission from: St Kilda Marina

Where will you keep it?

FORKLIFT
This photo is used with permission from St Kilda Marina

HARDSTAND
This photo is used with permission from St Kilda Marina

Don't look at this as additional expense; see it as an opportunity to make boating simpler and easier for the entire family. No I'm not advocating throwing money away, but I am into convenience and here's why…

So your boat is now at a marina or boat storage facility and costing you money, they should have adequate security in place to protect your boat and everyone else's. Your marina will also offer off-street car parking and member toilet/shower facility, which makes your time at the marina just a little more comfortable especially for the kids.

Keeping your boat in yard/dry storage is usually on a hard stand and out of the water. Ahh free from salt water, so she will definitely require a lot less maintenance and care, therefore saving you bucks (more on maintenance later).

If your boat is on a trailer, then the yard storage/dry storage will be for your hull only. So you'll need to find a place usually away from the marina to store your trailer. This may come as a cost, but maybe try a friend's office, warehouse, your garage, self-storage or even in your street. All will offer a place to keep her. If all else fails, some marinas will charge you

Where will you keep it?

an annual fee for storage of your trailer, if you have no other alternative.

Whatever you decide please don't sell your trailer even though it appears you won't need her anymore, now that she's stored at a marina. You may very well decide to take the boat away on holidays with you and you'll need a trailer for that. You may also decide to just keep the trailer for annual maintenance purposes enabling you to tow the boat to your favourite service centre or mechanic for repair and service. Maybe you just want to have the peace of mind in knowing your trailer is ready to go, whenever you are.

TIP: Remembering it's bloody hard to sell a trailerable boat without a trailer. It really narrows the potential market down when you decide to eventually sell the boat. Trailers can add significant cost to the price of a boat and buyers will get turned off having to add additional price their purchase. Besides, a seller will lose all negotiating strength if a buyer needs to factor a trailer purchase from elsewhere into the deal to make the numbers work. Keep your trailer, don't sell her without the boat - as most sellers usually regret the day they parted with their trailer.

Given that your boat is stored without a trailer, how will you get the boat launched and retrieved from her hardstand? A forklift usually operates at most marinas to offer this service without any additional charges (regardless of how many times your boat gets lifted) so please use it. Most owners say it's the best and most convenient way to go boating.

Typically you telephone the marina (during business hours) and ask for your boat to be launched at a specified time. Give them plenty of notice

Where will you keep it?

as they're always busy on the nice and wind-free boating days; remember every other owner is thinking the same thing as you. Please also leave your bung in the boat at all times. If you need to remove water from inside the hull after a wash or heavy rain, then replace the bung tightly when you're finished. Otherwise you may find she may not be launched by marina staff as they don't have time to search your boat for the missing bung.

> **TIP:** All marinas will have a policy/procedure request for BUNGS, so please make sure you discuss this issue with them at the beginning of your storage arrangement. It makes for a better boating experience if everyone understands what's required, besides a boat without bung, isn't really a boat, it's a rock. She will sink very quickly. Whilst most boat insurance policies will cover this accident, it is going to piss everyone off!

On those days where you're going boating, maybe for a fish at dawn, ask the marina to launch your boat just before they head home the night before. That way your boat is sitting in the water and ready to go when you arrive early, ready for your 4am hunt for snapper.

Remember when you return to wash her down and flush the engine as marina staff won't usually do this. So your boat is now being forked in and out of the water and you're not messing around with a trailer. Isn't this worth the extra expense? You'll use the boat more, just ask any boat owner at a marina. It's all about convenience and simplicity.

A noticeable past-time amongst hardstand boat owners is to send the kid's home with your spouse, open up a nice cold beer and enjoy the quiet me time of relaxation whilst you give the boat a good wash, tidy up the inside and get her ready for your next family outing.

TIP: Alternatively for those that want to share the load and teach the kids about responsibility associated with owning a boat, let your partner go home, or send them on a nice walk or to get a coffee, leaving you with the kids to help you wash and tidy up the boat together. This will teach them responsibility and good habits for owning their own boat someday. Besides, the more hands on deck, the quicker the task will be completed. Advice for you: please be clear with your instructions and assign tasks to your kids, give them some trust and teach them what to do and explain why it's important. They will eventually pick up the ball and complete their task without you asking.

Good parenting can be very rewarding, your boat will be better maintained and your relationship with your kids will improve dramatically and your spouse will have some free-time.

Yes, good life-lessons are to be gained from boat ownership.

In (Wet) Water Storage

So say the ultimate in boat ownership and convenience.

Imagine this....you arrive after a hard day at work to the marina paradise. Access to the member's car park is via swipe card so you have added piece of mind. It's hot and balmy; daylight savings ensures that activity

Where will you keep it?

along the coast is vibrant and exciting, late into the evening.

MARINA BERTH
This photo is used with permission from
St Kilda Marina

You park the car only metres from your boat; you jump on-board and change from wearing that suit and tie, for a pair of shorts and your favourite T-shirt. Whilst you're waiting for your spouse to arrive with the kids, you open a cold beer and smile.

Your family arrives and parks the car next to yours. The kids already out of school uniform, they are really excited to see their Dad plus go boating on a school night. You untie the mooring lines and motor out of the marina to head for your own piece of paradise not too far offshore.

Drop anchor and eat roast chicken and salad that your spouse grabbed on the way to the marina. You see boating is all about lifestyle; it's about using the available time we have to enjoy the moment. The moment where your mobile phone doesn't ring, your email inbox isn't alerting you, the PlayStation is nowhere in sight.

Where will you keep it?

This is the time to talk about what happened at school today, without interruptions and excuses.

You are in the outdoors spending quality time with your family or friends on the water.

Given it's a school night you don't need to be out for long, just long enough to reconnect, refocus and re-energise.

Perhaps you've' elected to go boating with a friend or even maybe alone. It can be hard to choose your activity; maybe it's to drop anchor in a secluded cove, have a fish or give the throttle a squirt. Whatever it is, it's now your time to enjoy the fruits of your labour and the wonderful benefits of boat ownership.

Life's Better with a Boat!

Having your boat stored on the water (wet-berth) is a great way to actually use your boat much more. Gone is every single reason why boating is inconvenient; why boating can be a hassle. Here you are with your boat sitting in the water, all day and every day at call. It is now really up to you, to make the time to use her. Remember you don't need all day, just even one hour, you'll feel so much better. With your own gate key and car park access 24/7, you come and go when you please.

The notion of an on-water holiday house or weekend apartment is now very real. Here you have your own boat, filled with your own clothing, food, favourite books and with everything just the way you want it, when you want it and how you want it. You boat could be used on the weekends and on holidays for you and your family to live for short-periods at the marina. State law often prevents living aboard as your permanent place of residence, so check with the authorities first, if that's your intention.

Where will you keep it?

Ladies, you must use your boat for regular lunchtime gatherings with your girlfriends. Each brings a plate or asks the café or restaurant at the marina to cater, most will be delighted to assist. Together with a few glasses of Champagne or a fruity Sauvignon Blanc, lunchtime becomes a lovely afternoon without even having to turn the engines on. With the boat safely tied up in her mooring, she is well-protected from the elements. So who cares about the weather as this activity is not weather dependant, it's terrific in the pouring rain.

Alternatively with fast internet and Wi-Fi access, you can be sitting aboard doing work on your laptop or iPad and no one will ever know. You can be talking to your customers and writing them an important proposal all completed whilst you're sitting on your boat. Surely that's got you thinking of the endless possibilities?

Private Jetty

For those who live on a water system perhaps in an apartment on the water's edge or a house on one of those terrific canal estates, then you may be one of the truly lucky ones to have a boat in your own backyard or on your own private jetty.

JETTY
This photo is used with permission from St Kilda Boat Sales

Consider an air-dock system, whereby your boat is raised out of the water and stored above the waterline. This means salt water is not touching your hull and will enhance your boat's appearance and longevity. This also reduces the costs of maintenance and antifoul (more about this later).

If you've got your own jetty then the type of boat you select will be more in keeping with what you intend to use her for. Given you already have all the creature comforts at home on the water's edge anyways, so an on-water apartment that we talked about earlier, may not work. Perhaps it's just a fishing style of boat that appeals, maybe a day-boat to explore local waterways or a ski boat to take the kids for a ski, tube or wake.

Swing Mooring

We tend to see swing moorings dotted down the coast at holiday destinations in coastal areas. Effectively, a swing mooring is a buoy anchored just off the coastline in deep enough water for your boat to float in all tides. The mooring is usually leased to the boat owner for an annual period and the costs are not usually expensive. A boat is attached to the buoy and allowed to swing in the wind and current and is stored there for prolonged periods such as all of summer. In winter the boat is put on her trailer and taken away for maintenance and storage. Most popular during the Christmas and New Year period along the coast, swing moorings do not offer any protection from the elements or the birds what-so-ever. So boats kept on swing moorings for prolonged periods, tend to be harshly treated and noticeably tired.

You usually paddle a small inflatable dingy or tinny to the mooring from the beach and get on-board. Then you bring the boat to shore to collect your guests and your provisions for your day on the water.

Where will you keep it?

SWING MOORING
This photo is used with permission from: Darren Finkelstein

Most boats are then taken out of the water for winter when they are maintained, cleaned and repaired. Antifoul is required, careful consideration should be given to battery charging, bird poo, boat cleaning and your covers.

7

What is the cost of boating?

How much coin is needed?

When you consider buying a boat, the price is usually the number one factor. But being able to afford the boat depends on more than the initial boat price, even if it's a great deal. Whether you are buying a new or used boat, consider all of these expenses when you set your boating budget.

Purchase Price

Everyone wants the best possible price on the items they purchase, and probably even more so, on a big-ticket item such as a boat. To be sure you get the best possible deal on a boat you will need to do your research and shop around. As mentioned in an earlier chapter, visit several Dealers/Brokers to get a sense of the range of prices for the model of boat you have chosen and jump on the internet to do a Google search.

If you are purchasing a used boat, *www.BoatPoint.com.au* and *www.BoatSales.com.au* list boat retail values, but they're only the "listed sell prices," so the actual purchase prices after negotiation will be much less. Another source for used boat pricing is to ask your Dealer/Broker for a valuation. Be sure it's based on the actual sell prices for similar or like models of the boat of your interest. This way you can get a direct comparison which is far more accurate. Since boats are like cars in the sense they depreciate quickly, your goal when purchasing a boat is to ensure you won't owe more than the boat is worth when you are ready to sell it.

Don't forget to include the cost of financing and insurance in your budget. Shop around for good loan rates, and get boat insurance quotes before you make the purchase (more on finance and insurance later).

Boat Operating Costs

Depending on the size and type of boat you buy, operating expenses will vary.

Fuel is easily the largest operating expense you will have. Estimate the boat's economical cruising speed or consult the boat specifications to get an idea of the fuel efficiency of the boat.

Boats that guzzle gas obviously will cost you more to operate, so you will need to consider this in your boating budget.

Other considerations when determining operating costs are storage costs and marina fees. If you plan to purchase a trailer boat and have a storage area at your home, paying for hardstand, yard or self-storage may not be an issue. If you intend to keep your boat in the water either at home or a marina, include these estimates in your boat operating budget.

Consider the cost of winterisation of your boat during the off-season when she will sit unused for a period of time. Boat engines are much like people; if you don't exercise, your muscles will get stiff and sore. Starting your engine allows parts to be lubricated, batteries to run and alternators to be charged. All of these important parts of the winterisation process

What is the cost of boating?

ensure longevity and reliability from your boat engine.

You will also need to include the annual registration fees for your boat and if you have one; the annual trailer registration fee. Both of these fees are payable annually to your state based registration authority. A registration transfer fee is also payable if you're buying a second-hand vessel. Also, in some states of Australia, stamp-duty is payable for a used boat and/or trailer purchase. So check with your local registration authority for details and costs. For a listing of all the registration authorities in Australia, read my later chapters.

Boat Maintenance Costs

Maintaining a boat costs money too, and like operating expenses, will depend upon the size and type of boat you buy. If you don't want to spend a lot of money on maintenance costs, purchase a low-maintenance boat - the simpler the better. A boat that doesn't require a lot of maintenance will be of simple construction requiring washing only and will be easy to repair. An oar-powered car-top style Tinnie is a perfect example of a low maintenance boat. Larger boats will require a bigger budget, and more time to maintain, but you and your family will get a greatly enhanced boating experience. Like everything in life, you get what you pay for and boats are no different!

One way to relieve maintenance costs is to do the work yourself if you are able and qualified. Whether you do the work, or you have your boat serviced, the basic boat maintenance costs to budget for are: cleaning supplies, engine and hull servicing, and emergency repairs.

Set a Boating Budget

Before you start shopping for a new boat, set a boating budget that includes all of the costs of owning a boat by taking everything into account.

This will help you choose a boat that matches your needs at a price within your budget.

Research and Compare Financing Options

You can finance a new boat just like a new car. As with car and home loans, boat loans have carried extremely appealing interest rates in recent years. Terms generally range from two to five years. Comparing rates online is a great starting point. Also, some lenders will offer up-to 50% balloon or residual payments on some leading boat brands such as: Caribbean, Bertram, Riviera, Maritimo and Sea Ray where they know the resale values will remain strong and the used market is very active.

Decide which Options and Accessories You Would Like to Have

Similar to new cars, new boats are offered with different accessories and options. When you're pricing boats, factor in the cost of electronics, accessories and water toys. Buy what's appropriate for your boat type, boat size and your home waters. Modern marine electronics are extremely reliable, loaded with features and more affordable than ever. Don't skimp on safety gear. Today's marine accessories can increase boating safety and fun, and make it down right easier than it was just a few years ago.

Service, Repair and Maintenance Costs

Did you know around 82% of all boating incidents reported last year were due to boats breaking down on the water? Maintenance doesn't have to be a chore! Get into the routine and maintain your boat, your safety depends on it....

What is the cost of boating?

Note of caution: The below service and ongoing costs are a guide only to give readers an understanding of what costs will be incurred as a result of purchasing a used boat. I strongly recommend you speak to your local service and repair centre to confirm charges and fees. You are most welcome to shop around, however my experience suggests the local repairers are all competitively priced. Typically they all have the same hourly rates and the basic service fees for engine service, repairs and parts. Warranty claims are usually set nationally by the actual engine manufacturer.

So if we remove the price from the equation for just a moment, the important factors for consideration when selecting your repairer include: location, convenience, facility, accreditation/qualifications. Ultimately what's really important is the relationship you build with the repairer. Most service and repair centres have loyal customers for many years, even when they change boats.

The majority of manufacturers for outboard, inboard, Sterndrive or Shaftdrive engines suggest engines be serviced annually or at 100 hour intervals, which-ever comes first. So regardless of whatever the engine manufacturer suggests in their marketing materials, all vessels used especially in salt water, must to be serviced annually - regardless of hours used! Stretching the service intervals longer can have detrimental effects to longevity and reliability of your engine.

TIP: Beware of people claiming they have only used the boat for "hardly any" hours last year. Boat engines especially used in salt water need to be run; otherwise moving parts, seals and piping can and will dehydrate and corrode. Therefore, regardless of the engine hours, if less than 100, service your boat annually. Fresh water run engines also need to be serviced annually, although they are less of a concern.

Annual Service Fees

Outboard

Costs vary greatly depending on the horsepower of engine. Below is an actual example of the typical Mercury Outboard labour rates, which have been determined and set by the actual engine manufacturer.

Up to 5hp	$148.50 plus parts
6-30hp	$247.50 plus parts
40-90hp	$346.50 plus parts
115-125hp	$396.00 plus parts
140-250hp	$445.50 plus parts
250hp +	check with your local service centre

Sterndrive

Circa $600.00 per engine block for labour plus parts, this will depend on the horsepower. The actual leg or drive unit also requires servicing, so please check with your repairer for the actual cost involved.

Shaftdrive

Circa $600.00 per engine for labour plus parts, this will depend on the horsepower and the engine make and model.

Additional information regarding engine service, repairs and vessel maintenance should be directed to the following:
- Engine Manufacturer – The engine handbook or owner's manual.
- Engine manufacturer's website.
- Your preferred repairer.

>  **TIP:** Ask the Boating Industry Association in your state or Marine Queensland, for a list of recommended marine trades who are industry association members that are either accredited or experienced in the particular discipline you are seeking e.g. engine service, repair, trimmings, fiberglass, antifoul, stainless steel, electronics, toilets, refrigeration, air conditioning etc.
>
> They would be delighted to help.

Antifoul

Wikipedia describes "Anti-fouling paint or bottom paint as a specialised coating applied to the hull of a ship or boat in order to slow the growth of organisms that attach to the hull and can affect a vessel's performance and durability". Hull coatings may have other functions in addition to their anti-fouling properties, such as acting as a barrier against corrosion on fibreglass, aluminium, timber and metal hulls.

Additionally, anti-foul improves the flow of water past the hull, which is of prime importance for all types of recreational and commercial boats. This especially applies for commercial vessels such as fishing trawlers, container ships, cruise liners or high-performance and competition racing boats where time is money and finishing the race first are all that matters.

However, for us recreational powerboat owners, keeping your hull clean and free from harsh build-up will increase your boat's performance and speed through the water and will increase your boat's longevity and reliability.

What is the cost of boating?

So don't think antifoul is only important to ocean liners, it's not and will be costly if you don't pay attention to the condition of your hull.

In the days of the clipper ships, sailing vessels suffered severely from the growth of barnacles and weed on the hull, called "fouling." Thin sheets of copper or Muntz metal were nailed onto the hull in an attempt to prevent marine growth. Fouling affected performance (and profitability) in two ways. First, the maximum speed of a ship decreases as its hull becomes fouled with marine growth. Second, fouling hampers a ship's ability to sail upwind.

The inventor of the anti-fouling paint was Captain Ferdinand Gravert, born in 1847 in Glückstadt (Schleswig-Holstein, now in Germany, but then Danish), who sold his chemical formula in 1913 at Taltal, Chile. Captain Alex Gravert has valuable documentation about this.

One famous example of the traditional use of metal sheathing is on the clipper Cutty Sark, which is preserved as a museum ship in dry-dock at Greenwich in England. A modern version of this anti-fouling system, Copper Coat, uses an epoxy resin to permanently attach copper to the hull of the boat, helping to prevent marine growth for ten years or more.

Largely dependent on your boat's storage location and water temperature, Antifoul is only required on boats that will be in the water constantly for a period longer than about 30 days. Up to 30 days you can easily remove the growth and build-up on the hull without causing any damage to the hull's integrity by pressure cleaning with water, followed by an acid wash, if your hull is stained.

Otherwise any period longer than 30 days will result in your hull needing to be sanded back or even sand blasted to ensure the removal of growth. If this is not done, the gelcoat (the protecting and shiny surface on the outside of a fibreglass boat) will be damaged permanently. The damage may result in the need for preparation, epoxy and Antifoul to be applied permanently. The resultant damage to timber and aluminium boats is

What is the cost of boating?

similar although the tell-tale signs can differ for fibreglass, so it pay's to get good advice and hire an industry professional to carry out the works for you. Don't try this yourself, unless you have experience, the right tools and know what you are doing.

For example, Antifoul is required in Victorian waters every 12-18 months; due to the low average water temperature as reported by *www.sea-temperature.com* as 17 degrees C. Interestingly, Queensland berthed vessels may require anti-foul every 6-8 months where the average water temperature is 25 degrees C.

A typical first-time Antifoul, for a new fibreglass boat or used boat that's never been Antifouled before, requires the following process:

1. Crane lift or yard slip (get the boat onto dry land).
2. Slip and pressure clean (to remove growth).
3. Apply epoxy primer (protects the hull just like Gelcoat).
4. Antifoul coating (several coats).

Below is a sample outline of total cost involved for undertaking the above –listed process:

- 26ft - $ 1,750
- 35ft - $ 2,700
- 45ft - $ 3,500

A first time Antifoul (for a new boat or hull never Antifouled) requires a significantly different process involving sanding and several coats of epoxy primer. Consequently, first-time Antifouls are more expensive, but thereafter for the re-Antifoul process, prices are a few hundred dollars cheaper.

A clean hull on your vessel will improve the speed of the vessel through the water and consequently, may reduce fuel consumption. A clean hull means less friction, therefore, cheaper to run. In addition, a propeller(s) without rough edges or damaged fins also improves the vessel's performance, handling and fuel consumption.

The Antifoul process usually takes about five days, depending on the weather so it's best to book in on a Monday, that way she will be back into the water on Friday, in time for your weekend's boating activity.

Sacrificial Anodes

Anodes are sacrificial by nature and are designed to dissolve in salt and fresh water. They are installed on a vessel under the waterline usually on or near the engine, rudder or trim tabs to attract electrolysis rather than the electrolysis attacking your very expensive propellers' and/or engine structure. Wikipedia says, "electrolysis is the passage of a direct electric current (DC) through an ionic substance that is either molten or dissolved in a suitable solvent, resulting in chemical reactions at the electrodes and separation of materials."

Therefore, it's your sacrificial anodes that will dissolve once the current attacks them. It's better than the electrical current attacking your propellers or other underwater structures on your boat. Due to the role they play anodes are a rather inexpensive consumable item that will need replacing regularly before they fully dissolve.

Outboard Engine

When dry stored on a trailer, the anodes will only need replacing when they have deteriorated and are usually circa $100 including fitting of them.

Sterndrive Engines

When wet-berthed anodes will require replacement circa four-five months.

What is the cost of boating?

Price includes: Slipping your boat to access the anodes which are attached to the Sterndrive unit. A pressure clean of your hull at the same time is usually required.

Total cost approx. $500 each time. This process may take two-three hours depending on the ability to pressure clean your hull.

Shaftdrive Engines

Usually requiring crane or travel-lift for access – Price on application from your local ship yard where the listing capability resides. Prices are typically fixed and club member discounts may apply. Depending on the size and quantity of your anodes and boat length, these are usually replaced only every 12-18 months or when an Antifoul occurs.

Some anodes for the larger vessels may be replaced by a scuba diver. Scuba divers are available through a marina or service provider. This process may take a few hours depending of the ability to hand scrub your hull and is usually a few hundred dollars plus the cost of the anodes.

Other Boat Maintenance

Boat maintenance doesn't have to be a chore – get into a routine and maintain your boat to prevent breakdown on the water. Below is a handy reference that the good folk at Transport Safety Victoria through their Maritime Safety Group, has put together. More information can be found at, *www.transportsafety.vic.gov.au.*

The four main areas to check:

Motor

Manufacturers usually recommend a service by a specialised workshop at least once a year- even if the motor is hardly used. This ensures vital internal parts such as the water pump are checked. If your motor is used regularly, you should change your gear-box oil every three months.

Also check the following;
- Replace your pull-cord if it is fraying.
- Wiring.
- Clean spark-plugs, check gaps and replace if required.
- Compression.
- Lubricate all moving parts.
- Re-fill gear case oil.
- Cooling system passages.
- Propeller and nut – sand or file any small cracks.
- Replace the sacrificial anode if required.

Fuel
- Always replace old fuel - never go out with fuel which is more than six months old.
- Make sure you have enough fuel for the trip - 1/3 out, 1/3 back and 1/3 in reserve.
- Clean your fuel tank at least once a year with a suitable solvent and dispose of old fuel responsibly.
- Inspect the fuel tank for cracks or corrosion.
- Always replace old fuel after periods of inactivity.
- Inspect fuel lines, manual priming bulb and connections for cracks and leaks clean out or replace fuel filter.
- For fuel disposal please make contact with your local council for details.

Batteries
- Top-up battery cells with distilled water and check each cell with a hydrometer.

What is the cost of boating?

- The battery should be charged at a rate that is suitable to the battery and should never be over-charged.
- Batteries should be secured in brackets.
- Battery terminals, cables and casing should be kept clean.
- Grease terminals regularly.
- Test all equipment that uses the battery.

Boat Structure

- Clean and paint your boat regularly.
- Inspect boat for corrosion and cracks.
- Ensure all bungs are suitable and in good condition.
- Check for water and fuel leaks.
- Check and grease drain flaps.
- Ensure bilges are clean and dry.
- Test steering for stiffness - oil cables with the correct lubricant.

We also recommend keeping the following items on board:

- Engine manual.
- Flywheel pull rope.
- Spare 'O' rings for fuel connector.
- New spark-plugs.
- Spark-plug spanner (or diesel injector spanner).
- Ratchet with extender and shifting spanner.
- Spare fuses, bung and shackle.
- Sharp knife, pliers and screwdrivers.
- Spare propeller nut, washer, split pins and socket for propeller nut.
- Steel wool to clean battery terminals.

- De-watering spray (RP7 or similar).
- Spare oil and funnel.
- Spare key and stop harness (kill switch lanyard).

Boat Insurance

Why you need it?

It's best to buy separate boat insurance, rather than adding your boat to your homeowner's policy. Many homeowners' policies limit or don't cover marine-specific risks, such as salvage work, wreck removal, pollution or environmental damage.

Insurance Factors

Insurers consider many factors when deciding whether or not to offer a policy. Almost any vessel can be insured— for a price! You just want to make sure the policy meets your needs.

Below are some of the elements that need to be disclosed to your insurer, for an insurance quote to be issued:
- Age of boat
- Length
- Value
- Speed
- Condition
- Type of boats

- Owners boating experience and claim history

Types of Boat Insurance

There are two basic types of boat insurance—"agreed value" and "market value." An "agreed value" policy covers the boat based on its value when supported by a written valuation from an approved valuer.

For example, Club Marine (Australia's largest pleasure craft insurer), offers the ability to choose between agreed value and market value to get the best possible cover to suit both your boat and your boating lifestyle.

With an extensive network of marine dealers and service centres at your disposal, simply take your boat in for a formal valuation to determine which option best suits your needs.

Club Marine's *agreed value* policy gives you confidence that in the case of a total loss, your boat is insured up to the value as agreed upon in the formal valuation.

Club Marine's *market value* policy in the event of a total loss, the value of your boat equals the sale value immediately before the loss occurred, which can be affected by current economic conditions, the buoyancy of the buying and selling markets and other factors which are outside the control of the person insured.

Types of Policies

Marine insurance covers a wide berth of watercraft. You may be surprised to find what can be insured. Marine insurance policies include:
- Boats.
- PWC / watercrafts.
- Yachts - Generally, vessels 26' and smaller are called "boats," and

"yachts" are 27' and larger. Yacht coverage tends to be broader and more specialised because larger boats travel farther and have more unique exposures.

- Sailboats
- Dinghy's
- Boats & PWC Rental – Although this is generally not required, rental insurance will help cover any damage to the vessel, as well as the operator and passengers. Ask your insurer for details regarding insurance for commercial vessels.
- Boat Club – Covers all members of club while operating a boat.
- Professional (ProAngler, Fishing Guides & Charters) – These policies are customisable and can cover items like travel to a tournament, equipment and more.

Learn the basics of boat insurance. Why you need it, what it includes and how to get it.

Types of Coverage

What Boat Insurance Policies Cover

For example, Club Marine's comprehensive insurance cover gives you complete peace of mind and protection to safeguard your boating lifestyle.

Club Marine's comprehensive insurance includes items that some other insurance providers may offer as add-ons at an additional charge. At Club Marine, they do seem to go the extra distance to give you and your boat complete cover that really is comprehensive.

Policy covers includes:
- Accidental loss, damage, fire and/or explosion and theft to your boat.
- Cover for liability to other people, including death or injury, and damage to their property.
- Club Marine Assist - 24 hour emergency assistance and personal service on and off the water.
- Choose between agreed or market value policies if your boat is less than 20 years old.
- Always there for you with 24/7 claims assistance.
- Cover for the discharge and escape of fuel, lubricant and sewage from holding tanks on your boat of up to $500,000.

Also available is your personal copy of Club Marine Magazine - Australasia's leading marine lifestyle magazine.

My duty of disclosure

Darren Finkelstein and St Kilda Boat Sales are authorised Platinum Dealers for Club Marine Insurance and receives a sales commission for insurance policies sold and renewed.

It is strongly suggest that you fully read the Product Disclosure Statement (PDS) and Financial Services Guide (FSG) for specific information regarding policy wording and insurance cover.

For details of Club Marine's comprehensive insurance, please speak to your local Club Marine Dealer, Insurance Broker or Club Marine directly *www.clubmarine.com.au*

What is the cost of boating?

Understanding those Special Conditions in your policy

Inboard Report

Inboard powered runabouts older than 10 years require an inspection report.

Custom-built boats and vessels of wooden or steel construction also require an inspection report, regardless of age.

Your local marine dealer or service centre will be able to perform the required inboard inspection and complete the report.

Condition Report

Outboard, Sterndrive and jet-powered runabouts and trailer sailors older than 20 years require a condition report. Custom-built boats and vessels of wooden or steel construction also require an inspection report, regardless of age.

Your local marine dealer or service centre will be able to perform the required inspection and complete the condition report.

TIP: Alternatively give the St Kilda Boat Sales Service Centre a call as we are an authorised Club Marine Platinum Dealer, Valuer and Repairer call (03) 9525-5500 or go to: *www.stkildaboatsales.com.au.*

If you're buying a used boat, your pre-purchase inspection will suffice, so make a photocopy and submit instead of a condition report.

Risk Evaluation & Survey Reports

Moored vessels older than 20 years require an inspection report.

Custom-built boats and vessels of wooden or steel construction also require these reports, regardless of age.

These reports can be completed by any Qualified Marine Surveyor or by a Local Shipwright.

Making an insurance claim

Hopefully, you will never need to make a claim but if you do, it's good to be prepared. You are not required to carry proof of insurance on your boat, but it's a good idea to keep claim information handy for an emergency. Ask how the claim process works when you're shopping for policies. Ideally, it should be quick and easy. In addition, find out if your agent (or other representative) will be available if you need help dealing with the aftermath of a claim, such as arranging for towing or salvage, rather than just cutting a check and leaving.

Find out what kind of coverage you want based on your needs.

Boat Insurance Cost

Shopping for Boat Insurance

Start with a little fact-finding. Ask your boating friends which company they use, and how their claims have been handled. The way an insurer has handled claims in the past is a good indicator of the quality of service you can expect in the future.

Go to a boat show and talk without obligation to the exhibitors. Find out what's what.

Policy Discounts

There are a few ways to reduce your boat insurance costs. If your boating is restricted by seasons (usually called lay-up), for example; your boat is in storage during the winter, you can get deductions for winter layup.

Many insurers offer discounts for good driving records (no claim-bonus discounts) and for those who have completed boater education classes or are club members.

Finally, multi-policy discounts do apply, so if you have a PWC and wish to ensure a powerboat, then an additional discount will apply.

How to Pay

The choice of payment is typically:
- Annually with credit card (Club Marine offers 5%).
- Pay by the month insurance is available. Typically adding a small service fee to the transaction of about 7%.
- Direct Debit.
- Cash via your dealer or broker.

So in summary, what is the total cost of ownership? Use my worksheet below to calculate the total cost of ownership. Remember this worksheet is provided as a guide only and the outcome will give an approximate indication only.

What is the cost of boating?

Actual Purchase Price of your boat $

Plus

Transfer Fee - Used Boat (if applicable) $

Transfer Fee - Used Trailer (if applicable) $

Stamp Duty- Used Boat (if applicable) $

Stamp Duty- Used Trailer (if applicable) $

Annual Registration - New Boat (if applicable) $

Annual Registration - New Trailer (if applicable) $

$ **a.**

Annual Fees

Registration (Boat) $

Registration (Trailer) $

Comprehensive Insurance for pleasure craft $

$ **b.**

What is the cost of boating?

Storage	$
At home	$ no charge
Self-Storage	$
Friends (home or office)	$
Marina (trailer park, hardstand, wet-berth)	$
Club Membership (if required)	$
	$ c.

Maintenance & Insurance (annual)

Trailer Service	$
Engine Service	$
*Anodes (includes Pressure Clean & Slip)	$
*Antifoul (includes Pressure Clean & Slip)	$
Misc. Repairs	$
Boat Washing, Cleaning and Polishing	$
Boat Insurance	$
	$ d.

Remember - This is based on your water temp, so please calculate The annual cost based on the length of time that your anodes & antifoul last. For the sake of ease, you may want to assume that your antifoul lasts for 12 months.

What is the cost of boating?

Running Costs

Fuel Cost (by consumption) $

Electricity Costs (shore power) $

                                                _____

                                                _____

                                                $ e.

Total – All annual costs as listed above $
(add: b + c + d + e)

Divide your boat purchase price by say 5 $
(assuming you plan to keep boat for 5 years)

*Total cost of Ownership over 5 years $_____

For some boat buyers and boat owners, both the cost of boat finance and depreciation may need to be included in this calculation for accuracy purposes. It is important to realise and note that other factors will change the outcome shown above and influence the cost of ownership as calculated.

Disclaimer: This information is put together as nothing more than a guide for illustration purposes only.

A professional financial advisor should be sought to better understand and determine if an actual boat purchase is truly affordable for you, given your individual financial circumstances.

8

How to BUY a boat.

How to buy the right boat at the right price.

Congratulations so you have decided to buy a boat. Well-done, good times are ahead for you and your family.

For some buyers, they will just love the opportunity to search for a suitable boat knowing they have their partner's approval to buy. They enjoy going from marina to marina, visiting boat dealers, buying magazines, and researching the internet. Others don't like it at all and just want to get on the water, without all the mucking around.

As a reminder, its important when buying a boat that you refer to these questions and you should have clear answers to them in your mind;

1. What are your main reasons for wanting a boat?
2. What is your shortlist of boat types? (New or Used)
3. Where is your preferred storage location?

Remember, educated and knowledgeable buyers find the process of buying a boat a whole lot easier and will get a better DEAL than those who don't prepare or know exactly what they are looking for to suit their needs!

NEW Boat Buyers

The idea of buying a NEW boat makes the purchasing process a lot more focused because you'll only need to identify the authorised and appointed dealers for the specific brand or make of boat that takes your interest. If you don't know, then visiting a Boat Show is a must!

In Australia our distribution networks for boat manufacturers are really clear and simple. Google has the answers for everything, so jump on the internet and find out who is the local dealer of your preferred brand of boat. Visit the dealer and find out what's available.

Furthermore, ask what's included as standard fixtures, fitting options and accessories from the manufacturer. Also ask what options are available from both the manufacturer and selling dealer. Grab a retail pricelist and study it well. Select what your preferred options and accessories are so you can have them fitted to your boat. Armed with an accurate idea of what you are looking for, create a list of these items and give them to the dealer. Then ask for a detailed proposal/quotation in writing. Understand that the best DEAL you will get is at the time of purchase, it makes sense that the more fixtures, fitting options and accessories you select in your boat package - the bigger the discount will be, because the dealer has more margin in the total deal.

Therefore, a smart buyer knows this is a great opportunity for negotiating a ripper deal. With more margins in the deal, there's more discount to pass onto you as the buyer. Therefore it stands to reason the more basic your new boat purchase is, the less margin the dealer has to play with, therefore the smaller the discount you'll receive. It might sound a bit

How to BUY a boat

confusing at first read through – so don't panic too much.

For those Caribbean new boat buyers either for; Trailerable Runabout

or a Cruiser, a great feature of my website is what we call Option-A-Boat. This unique feature has been really popular amongst boat buyers at all different price ranges and gives you the ability to build a new boat from scratch by selecting your options and accessories available from a large database of choices available to that specific Caribbean boat model.

Online Boat Creation

Created exclusively by St Kilda Boat Sales, our exclusive Option-A-Boat online quoting system lets you price your new Caribbean Boat by selecting your engine, electronics, covers, fishing equipment and many other options and accessories. After registration, your formal quote will be emailed to you within minutes.

www.stkildaboatsales.com.au/option-a-boat

As part of your research phase, find out from the boat manufacturer exactly how their distribution model in Australia works.

TIP: Find out if an interstate boat dealer can actually sell a NEW boat outside their home state border. E.g. Can a Perth based client (holding a WA Drivers or Boat License) buy a NEW boat from say, a Sydney dealer? Importantly, also be sure to ask the process for warranty claims and for after-sales service. And finally ask how the service would be carried out if the boat is in a different state to the selling dealer.

Why ask about interstate boat dealers in the first place? Some leading Australian boat manufacturers will NOT let their dealers sell a NEW boat outside of the dealers' home state. It's like a sales territory, with geographic limitations so it's best to check with the actual boat manufacturer first.

Consequently, it's your local dealer you need to build a relationship with for sales, service and advice through your boat ownership. Besides, if you want to get a ripper DEAL, then it pays to build a good relationship with them anyway!

Look on the bright side when it comes to local service and local support, its obvious the local dealer can easily assist. It's more convenient to tow your boat on her trailer or drive the boat on water to the selling dealer to be repaired or fixed whilst it's under warranty.

It comes down to good-old fashioned service and to the local dealers' ability to look after you! After the warranty has expired, you can take your boat anywhere you like for service, repair and assistance.

Remember to focus on service and not just price alone, although price is important too. It's important to build long-term relationships with your local dealers as most people stick with the selling dealer through multiple boat ownerships, if their experience is positive and customer expectations are constantly met.

Boat Shows

The Australian boating community has a wonderful choice of boat shows across the entire nation that showcases the latest technology and the newest models for you to inspect, climb over, sit in and admire:

The Aussie Boat Show season is typically as follows:

How to BUY a boat

February	**Melbourne International Boat & Lifestyle Show**	
	Melbourne, Victoria	
	www.biavic.com.au	
March	**Brisbane Tinnie & Tackle Show**	
	Brisbane, Queensland	
	www.tinnieandtackle.com.au	
May	**Sanctuary Cove International Boat Show**	
	Sanctuary Cove, Queensland	
	www.sanctuarycoveboatshow.com.au	
July	**Melbourne Boat Show**	
	Melbourne, Victoria	
	www.biavic.com.au	
June	**Adelaide Boat Show**	
	Adelaide, South Australia	
	www.adelaideboatshow.com.au	
August	**Sydney International Boat Show**	
	Sydney, New South Wales	
	www.sydneyboatshow.com.au	
August	**Brisbane Boat Show**	
	Brisbane, Queensland	
	www.brisbaneboatshow.com.au	
October	**Club Marine Mandurah Boat Show**	
	Mandurah, Western Australia	
	www.mandurahboatshow.com.au	
November	**Gold Coast Marine Expo**	
	Gold Coast Marine Precinct, Queensland	
	www.gcmarineexpo.com.au	

According to the Boating Industry Association of Victoria's (BIAV), "The Melbourne Boat Show attracts a large number of people from the general public with an interest in purchasing a new boat or simply upgrading, as well as those looking for a great deal on fishing and marine accessories."

"We also find the Show an excellent venue for educating the public about some of the biggest issues at the moment regarding buying vessels, and that is undoubtedly grey imports. People just aren't aware of the risks involved in buying a grey import".

TIP: Grey market or grey import also known as parallel market - is the trade of a commodity through distribution channels which, while legal, are unofficial, unauthorized, or unintended by the original manufacturer. Remember it's the actual owner of the grey import which is fully responsible for that vessel and/or trailer and the onus is on them in regard to registration and local compliance, which is often difficult..

Boat shows offer a great place to walk around and view all of the different types of boats as I've outlined in my earlier chapter. The boats can be viewed all under one roof or out in the open at a single venue. So there is less running around to find what you're interested in.

As you walk around to view the boat choices, make notes of what you like and what you don't like in boat design, functionality and price. Come up with your preferred choices and try to match them as close as possible.

Things you must know, before you buy a Used Boat

Buy from a reputable dealer/broker who should be an "Accredited Boat Dealer/Broker."

Below is the Boating Industry Association explanation of Accreditation.

What is Accreditation?

Accreditation is a recognised standard that many industry bodies apply for to promote the fact that their business is of a higher standard with checks and controls in place to deliver a quality product or service. In many cases government only award contracts to accredited businesses. To the purchasing public, accreditation suggests higher quality, better service, reliability and peace of mind when using their products or service. Accreditation is recognised in the form of International Standards Organization (ISO) standards.

What are the Standards?

The standards focus is on customer satisfaction and achieving consistent quality of your services (or products). To get there, you set up, use and improve a 'quality management system' - i.e., the system you use to manage the quality of your services and/or products.

Getting Finance - Borrowing money to buy

You may want to pre-qualify for a boat loan before you shop. This will give you some extra leverage and breathing room when you're negotiating prices for a super deal. Why not organise a finance approval in advance for the style of boat you are thinking of buying? Having the finance in place ahead of time ensures you're ready to buy when the right boat comes along.

www.BoatPoint.com.au leading Australia classified website writes to their boat buyers about boat finance:

"Buying a boat whether large or small is a major investment to make, so, the manner in which you do that and with whom you decide to fund your purchase through deserves due consideration.

Boat lending is broken into two main areas - finance for commercial use and finance for personal use.

Credit providers give you immediate use of the vessel you choose in exchange for regular repayments made over an agreed period of time, after the final payment has been made clear, title passes to you".

In general, some of the features you can expect with your finance contract are:

- Payments will be structured to suit your budget and or needs.
- Finance terms - range from one year to five years.
    o Fixed repayments allow for your budgeting needs and protect you against interest rate fluctuations.
- A deposit is generally not required. Alternatively if a deposit is made then a reduction in repayments, interest and terms will be the major benefits.
- If your boat is to be used for business purposes you may qualify to claim part of the interest and depreciation as a tax deduction.
- Equity in your marine purchase can be increased, by making additional payments.
- Direct debiting of your monthly repayments can be arranged.
- Funding can be agreed to in advance giving you the ability to negotiate from a position of strength.

How much should you borrow?

As with buying a house or a car, some people may need to arrange finance to buy a boat. But before buying a boat, you need to establish your budget. The ability to redraw against property equity is a simple way to finance your boat purchase, if you choose.

You must ask your financial advisor first and calculate an affordable budget for your family. There is no point in you borrowing money to buy a boat you truly can't afford. Any enjoyment you hope to receive will only be significantly dissolved by the additional stress placed on you to meet repayments and up keep of the boat of your dreams. The dream may soon turn into a nightmare.

Boat Insurance

You probably bought your boat for fun and when you think of FUN, the last word that comes to your mind may be INSURANCE.

But of all the money you spent and will continue to spend on your pleasure craft, insurance may be some of the most crucial dollars that you spend. All other thoughts about insurance aside – some marinas will not even allow you to store your boat without adequate insurance. These include; St Kilda and Sandringham in Melbourne, Hillary's in Perth and the entire national D'Albora Marine group.

Safety Gear and Equipment

Do not assume safety gear or safety equipment is included in the purchase price of a boat and trailer that you've seen advertised, besides the location of where your actually boating determines what specific type of safety gear and safety equipment is needed to be carried on-board. So don't assume your compliance.

Private sellers will usually include in the sale, all of the safety gear they have with the boat regardless of whether it's actually compliant or even whether it's in good working condition. Boat dealers and brokers typically don't supply safety gear whatsoever with the purchase of any USED vessel. Largely because they are unable to guarantee the item's performance or condition, in an emergency situation.

Therefore, it is the purchasers' own responsibility to ensure full compliance. The current list of compliant, "Safety Equipment for Recreational Vessels," as published by the various government authorities, should be available from your local dealer/broker. I would suggest you get a copy and carefully read it to ensure your full compliance.

Most NEW boat dealers/brokers would be delighted to supply you with a new safety pack suitable for your exact boat type as part of your new boat purchase. Otherwise, buyers can purchase their own safety gear and safety equipment from a suitable chandler or applicable retailer.

Occasionally, when buying a used boat, an appreciative vendor sometimes leaves items such as safety gear, life jackets, flares, first-aid kits, ropes and fire extinguishers on the vessel for the new buyer to have at no-charge.

It should be understood this is as a gift and sometimes those items left aboard have already expired or do not work as well as they should e.g. batteries dead, lifejacket zippers broken or torn, flares expired, so please check.

TIP: Consequently, before taking a boat on the water, we strongly advise the purchaser to fully check those items left on-board, to ensure all items including; safety gear is in safe, compliant and operational condition. All items must also be checked to ensure that they have not reached their "use by" or "expiry date." Take your children to a professional chandler and have their life jackets properly fitted by a marine professional. It's important the children's life jackets do not slip overhead when they enter the water. Therefore good-fitting jackets are a mandatory buy for all of the kids. Also buy a few extras for friends when they come boating with you.

You are again reminded, that all such items left on-board by the vendors shall be taken with all defects and faults of description without any allowance or abatement whatsoever so please check the operation and just don't assume they are in good working order, I simply can't stress this enough.

Registration

Generally speaking, if your boat has a motor, it will need to be registered. The technical registration requirements registration fees and stamp-duty on transfers for each state differ.

Registering your boat (vessel) in Australia is a relatively straightforward process but because it does differ from state to state, I suggest you make contact with your local registration authority to check your local requirements, compliance, fees and charges before you purchase.

Boat trailers are often treated as vehicles; therefore your local motor-vehicle registration authority will handle all towing related questions and trailer regulations. Please contact them for your specific questions.

Who is your local boating authority?

New South Wales
Maritime NSW   Ph: 13 12 56
                                www.maritime.nsw.gov.au

Victoria
Vic Roads   Ph: 13 11 77
                                www.vicroads.vic.gov.au

South Australia
Transport, Travel & Motoring   Ph: 13 10 84
                                www.sa.gov.au

Tasmania
Marine & Safety Tasmania   Ph: 1300 135 513
                                www.mast.tas.gov.au

Queensland
Maritime Safety Queensland   Ph: (07) 3120 7462
                                www.msq.qld.gov.au

Western Australia
Department of Transport   Ph: 1300 362 416
www.transport.wa.gov.au

ACT
Recreational craft do not currently require registration.

Northern Territory
Recreational craft do not currently require registration, but check in case regulations have changed since publishing this book.

Making an Offer to Purchase

The process and strategy for making an offer is the same regardless of whether you're buying a boat directly from the owner under a private sale arrangement or from a dealer/broker.

A professional dealer/broker can help their buyer decide on a realistic offer range, which usually increases the chances of buying a pre-owned boat for a fair and reasonable price to both the vendor and buyer alike and with the necessary elements to protect your interests.

> **TIP:** Remember the dealer/broker will get a fee for selling the vessel (at a price that is acceptable to the vendor) so as long as you are aware of this potential conflict of interest upfront. A smart buyer will use this to their advantage, because they realise the dealer/broker will only get paid his fee if the boat sells. Therefore, the dealer/broker will be keen to make the sale happen, to get paid their commission.

An offer (unlike a solicitation) is a clear indication of the offeror's willingness to enter into an agreement under specified terms. The offer is made in a manner that a reasonable person would understand its acceptance and will result in a binding contract.

What's in an Offer?

Offers normally include a closing date, otherwise a period of 14 days after the date of offer is commonly assumed.

Like any negotiations, it is not where you start, but where you finish that is important. It's important that if you really want to buy the boat your negotiation tactics are friendly, respectful and not aggressive. Being aggressive may turn off a seller and you'll lose their desire to communicate or find a comfortable resolution for all, thus agreeing to the price. Remember any good negotiation is a win/win result for everyone!

Terms and conditions under which an offer is made, such as:
- Price
- Delivery Date
- Subject To:
    o Finance on/or before (insert date).
    o Satisfactory Pre-Purchase Inspection by a qualified person at the buyer's expense on/or before (insert date).
    o Satisfactory Hull Inspection by a qualified person at the buyer's expense on/or before (insert date).
    o Satisfactory Sea-Trial.
    o Validation of Service History.
    o Marina Berth or storage allocation/availability at buyer's expense.

So in terms of locking down a vendor, your Accredited Dealer/Broker will ask the buyer to make a formal offer for submission to the vendor (ideally in writing) which confirms the following:
- Price to be paid.
- Deposit payment which must be held in a "trust-styled account" until settlement.
- Settlement & Handover (date when final monies to be paid).
- Special Conditions such as: "subject to".

How to BUY a boat

Typically your Accredited Dealer/Broker will call the vendor (or forward an email) to advise them of the offer received from the buyer, at which time:

1. the dealer/broker will discuss the offer in detail, who then;
2. Makes a recommendation to the vendor, outlining what strategy to adopt, which will be based on overall buyer interest for the boat during the sales campaign and compare the offer to the vendor's expected price range. This will be based on discussions between the seller and the dealer/broker.
3. The vendor can either:
   a. Accept the offer.
   b. Ask for more money.
   c. Change the 'subject to' conditions
   d. Decline the offer and explain why.

To most experienced boat Dealers/Brokers, offers are not offers if they do not answer the above questions. Simply because once the vendor agrees, buyers are expected to sign contracts and pay deposits without hesitation.

Dealer/Broker credibility with a vendor is ultimately about TRUST, so any breaches or grey areas will cause difficulty in the relationship moving forward.

Buyers should have their purchase money ready or have their finance pre-approval in place, before making an actual offer.

> **TIP:** Buyers should be reminded that it's easier for vendors to accept their offer if their offer is simple, clean and without too many "subject to" conditions.

However unless you're buying a NEW boat or used boat that is still under warranty and you're convinced the warranty is transferrable, all buyers should insist on including the following clause:

Suggested Wording: *"Subject to a satisfactory pre-purchase inspection of hull, engine and sea-trial, carried out by a suitably qualified marine professional at the buyer's expense, on or before xx/xx/xx" (insert date)"*.

Pre-Purchase Inspection

All buyers in today's market must ask for an independent pre-purchase inspection to uncover and eliminate any potential surprises with their boat purchase. Most buyers should find out the exact condition of their intended purchase, before they commit to contract.

Given that most USED boat purchases are not covered by dealer warranty, bearing in mind that it is NOT a statutory requirement for boat dealers/brokers to offer any warranty with a used boat purchase whatsoever (unlike the car industry), it is strongly advised that the buyer hire the professional services of a qualified marine surveyor and/or mechanic during the purchase process and to thoroughly check the particulars and safe vessel operation.

The purchaser should inspect the vessel and/or trailer to satisfy them as to its sea and/or roadworthiness, condition, specification & Australian Builders Plate (ABP) compliance.

> **TIP:** The Boating Industry Association strongly recommends that for vessels that are over 15 years old and/or powered by petrol carburettor engines, a mechanical inspection be sought.

To find a suitably qualified, independent marine professional to undertake your inspection, please contact the Boating Industry Association in your state or ask your selling boat dealer/broker, they should be able to recommend a few suitable people.

Boat dealers/brokers who have service and engine repair facilities or workshops should not offer to undertake an inspection as this may be considered a conflict of interest and not really independent.

A boat dealer/broker should not receive any form of payment whatsoever, for recommending a particular inspection person.

Results of Inspection

The independent pre-purchase inspection has been carried out at the buyer's expense so everyone is keen to understand the findings. The next steps in the process will be dependent on the results of the inspection, below is the suggested course of action.

Pass – No faults or problems

Terrific, now agree on a settlement date. Your dealer/broker will now complete registration transfers for both boat and trailer in readiness for settlement and also a Statutory Declaration for the vendor's (seller's) signature which will need to have a suitably qualified person sign as witness to the vendor's signature.

Private buyers will also need to do this and may need to create a Statutory Declaration for the seller to sign. Most sellers may not actually know of this requirement, which is for the buyers benefit and protection anyway.

You will need to email or countersign the purchase papers to confirm you're now satisfied with the test and you agree to buy the boat "unconditionally".

Pass – But things are identified as faulty

Obtain a copy of the inspection report for your file and have a good read. Now you'll need to decide whether you still want to go-ahead with the purchase or not. Typically this will depend on the level and significance of the faulty items and of course the cost of repairs.

Through your Dealer/Broker, ask the buyer what they plan to do. Is this something that between the buyer and the vendor can be worked out to everyone's comfort? Maybe you could split the cost of repairs? Maybe the vendor can pay for the repairs in total, possibly because your offer was higher than you originally put forward. All these are feasible solutions, so work through the issues, maybe compromise is needed.

Ideally you should gain an idea from a qualified marine mechanic as to the approximate (even actual) cost of the repairs to the faulty items. Facts are easier to work with and it's much better than speculation.

Some buyers may see this opportunity to use this as a tool for gaining additional discount off the purchase price from a vendor. Maybe (and not forgetting) the buyer's actual purchase price was really low, so maybe the seller can't discount any further.

Whatever the result, buyers and sellers will need to agree and it's best to do it in a mature manner, without aggression. Remember a win/win result is best for everyone.

Sometimes you can't agree to work this out to every one's satisfaction, therefore you don't really have any other choice but to ask for a refund of your deposit as under the terms of the subject to clause given your pre-purchase inspection was NOT satisfactory.

Fail Test – Worst Case:

This is a really tough and difficult area to try and resolve.

But ultimately if the boat has simply failed its test and the reasons are now formally documented on the pre-purchase inspection report, usually the buyer will now be scared off.

In most cases, the seller doesn't really have any other choice but to refund the buyer's deposit under the terms of the subject to clause, given your pre-purchase inspection was NOT satisfactory.

TIP: As outlined in my later chapter: How to SELL a boat, I take time to outline the importance of getting the boat and trailer serviced before listing her for sale. In the above instances, if the seller would have done so before listing for sale, then the sale may have gone ahead.

Remember, everything comes out in the open when your boat and/or trailer are inspected at the request of an interested and genuine buyer. Non-disclosure of known issues and problems by sellers **always** gets found out in the long run during an inspection. So seller honestly saves everyone's time and energy and makes for a cleaner and quicker resolution for all parties.

Deposit Payments

When buying a boat, ensure you are prepared to leave a decent deposit. The deposit is required by law to complete one of the legal requirements for a contract to be activated. If you're unsure ask a lawyer for an explanation of contract law.

A decent deposit is usually 10% of the purchase price, which is not essential, but it's preferred. I recommend that a deposit be any amount that is enough to make an impact on the seller, so you may negotiate a better buy price. Anything's worth a try in a negotiation!

A boat dealer/broker must hold the deposit monies in a trust-styled account, which is a legal requirement until the purchase is paid in full and all monies are released. Tax Invoices and receipts will be issued.

If you're buying a boat privately, get the seller to give you a receipt for your payment and make sure all the relevant details including: engine numbers, the boat's HIN, the trailers VIN, registrations for both etc. are noted.

Settlement and Handover

Given that most of us bank online, settlement may be carried out when your private seller or boat dealer/broker receives payment for the boat and trailer in full.

Bank or personal cheques are not usually accepted as final payment unless the boat dealer/broker or private seller knows the buyer personally, so ask and seek clarification. Technically both bank and personal cheques can be cancelled and don't clear when deposited into your account for at least 3-5 days, therefore your private seller and Dealer/Broker won't release the boat & trailer until those funds are cleared and verified by their bank.

Internet or bank transfers are the simplest method and can be arranged between banks for a fee, so ask your personal or business banker to assist.

Finally remember to ensure that there are no monies owing by the seller to any finance company, lender or the like. I strongly recommend that you get a Statutory Declaration prepared and signed by the seller to confirm the boat and trailer is to be sold unencumbered and with clear-title. Ensure you receive it prior to settlement or don't settle until you have it in your hand.

If there is money owing, ask for written confirmation that the finance company agrees to sell with clear-title as no monies owing. Alternatively you can pay out the finance company at settlement and then give the balance of funds (equity) to the seller. If there is still a shortfall at settlement, being the payout figure is greater than the purchase price, then make sure the seller tops-up the balance first, before you settle; otherwise you are not buying with clear-title. In that case, you should not proceed with this purchase.

Handover is when the boat keys are given to the buyer at which time the private seller or Dealer/Broker should go through the operation of the boat with the buyer.

You'll want to understand where the battery switches are located and want a thorough overview, as your safety and enjoyment will greatly depend on your understanding of the boat's operation.

As this point in time, arrange to have some professional boat handling lessons for you and your family. It's really important that you and your family feel safe, confident and comfortable when out on the boat. If you're buying from Dealer/Broker they will be able to arrange this for you as part of their service. Alternatively, you can contact your local Volunteer Coast-Guard or Boat Club; they should be able to recommend the right person. I'd suggest a few lessons in different conditions will help to fine tune everyone's skills.

> **TIP:** It's a real bonus at settlement if the private seller or Dealer/Broker hands over the boat owner and operations manuals, service records, copies of registration papers and anything else that is available.
>
> Obviously the engine and cabin keys are not a bonus, they're mandatory along with signed registration transfers for both boat and trailer. Don't forget the Statutory Declaration as outlined earlier.

A tax invoice showing you have paid in full is also required - especially if you're an interstate buyer who will need to re-register the boat and trailer in your home state. At the time of registration all payments including transfer of registration, stamp-duty and other fees and changes are the responsibility of the buyer, so it's best to speak to your local registration authority and find out the process and costs first.

Payments to (Vendors) Sellers at Settlement

At settlement the buyer will pay the private seller directly (cash or bank transfer) this should have already been agreed and discussed.

However, if you're buying through an Accredited Dealer/Broker you will need to transfer the purchase price into their nominated account. The funds received should be of no surprise if you know the actual agreed selling price for which would have been discussed with you during the negotiation process.

Remember: *There is no cooling off period, so make sure you read and understand your contractual obligations as listed on your Offer To Purchase Contract.*

If not discuss them with the Dealer/Broker and don't sign anything until you're comfortable If you're still unsure, you should seek legal advice.

9

Buyer Beware

Learning from others, so you don't get it wrong.

Boat buyers regularly visit boat dealers and service centres all over the country, frustrated their boat purchase hasn't quite worked out the way they had planned. In some cases the exercise has blown-up into a potentially costly situation caused by dishonesty and riddled with broken promises.

Thankfully, not all boat purchases go this way, but no doubt the best way to enjoyably buy a boat without being ripped off or mislead is to buy from an Accredited Dealer of the Boating Industry Association, Marine Queensland or at least a financial member if there isn't an Accredited Dealer in your location.

Grey Imports - Buyer Beware

So what is a grey import?

With the Australian dollar currently tracking so high against the US dollar and with so much talk about buying stuff "cheaply" from the USA given their current financial situation, the notion of importing a new or used boat from the USA directly, without going through the authorized

Australian dealer network, offers much excitement and glamour to some buyers. Others are researching the possibilities, but buyers should be careful.

Marine dealers and brokers are authorized to sell specific product brands in Australia. This product must comply with Australian standards. Product which is sold through non-authorised channels is known as a "grey or parallel import."

Grey (or parallel) imports may seem very cheap on the surface. However, like most things that seem too good to be true; imported product may be far from cheap when compliance issues need to be addressed.

Marine Queensland the not-for profit industry authority for all things boating and marine, has put together this wonderful outline and explanation of Grey Imports. For more information, go to: *www.marineqld.com.au*

You're the importer - You're responsible.

By importing a boat, personal water craft (PWC) or engine into Australia, you are taking on a number of additional liabilities. You become responsible, personally, for all the compliance issues associated with the product.

In the event of a failure - be it safety or related to build standards or emissions - YOU will be the one, as the importer, bearing sole liability for compliance. In the event of an accident the skipper and/or owner of the vessel may carry very serious liability under Australian law.

Can you afford to take the risk?

Is it Safe?

Grey Imports raise both financial and safety concerns for buyers. As these products are being imported without the manufacturer's consent they will not be covered by the manufacturer's warranty. Grey imported products may not be subjected to the same thorough safety check that authorised products are subjected to. This means you could potentially be putting your family and yourself at risk through use.

It is important to remember that whilst the product may meet the safety requirements in its country of origin it does not mean that it will meet the minimum safety requirements here in Australia.

Is it Legal?

Products are manufactured for specific markets (or regions). This product is manufactured to comply with standards and specifications of each market.

Product which is imported into Australia must be assessed against Australian Regulations and Standards.

Much of the product currently being imported is NOT compliant. Australian Regulations and Standards are there for a reason. Non-compliant product needs to be viewed as substandard unless measures are taken to bring it into compliance. If a product cannot be brought into compliance it should not be sold, imported or even used within Australia.

Is it Worth It?

Have you given careful consideration to the true costs of importing a boat, PWC or engine? There is more to it than the price on the window.

After Sales Support

Most Authorised Dealers and Brokers are not permitted to provide after sale support such as servicing or spare parts to grey imports. This often means that any servicing and maintenance cannot be performed by factory trained professionals.

Resale

Grey and parallel imports often have very low or no value at the time of resale when compared to authorised products.

Product liability

Consumer advisories such as product safety recall and warranty supports are covered through Authorised Dealers and Brokers; however, unauthorised channels often do not.

Many insurance companies will not cover a claim if the product is found to be non-compliant against Australian standards. You could be uninsured.

Check the total cost of bringing the product into the country - you might be surprised to find there are costs and taxes in addition to the purchase price.

What Should You Look For?

Key compliance issues you should consider when evaluating imported products manufactured for overseas markets:

For Boats:

- Electrical Safety Compliance. All electrical systems must comply with Australian Standards and Regulations. "Certified Safe" does not equal compliant.
- Build specifications such as floatation standards, build standards and safety compliance - check to see that Australian Standards

are being complied with. If an accident occurs the skipper and/or owner of the vessel may carry very serious liability under Australian law.

For Engines (inboard/outboard motors, jet skis and electronic equipment):

- C-tick Certification under the Australian Communications Management Authority. This is a mandatory requirement for product sold in Australia.

For Trailers:

- Australian Design Rule (ADR) Compliance. No trailer is permitted on Australian roads unless it complies with this rule.

Why buy from an Authorised Dealer?

When you purchase your new boat, PWC or engine you can be assured that:

- You will receive full after sales support including warranty support, servicing and maintenance.
- Your product will comply with the standards and specifications unique to the Australian market.
- Your product will meet Australian Build Specifications including floatation standards, build standards and safety compliance.
- All electrical systems will comply with Australian Standards and Regulations.
- All products will possess C-tick Certification.
- Your trailer will be Australian Design Rule compliant.

- You will own a quality product, provided by a quality dealer AND be free to enjoy quality time on the water without the worry of what may go wrong with your "cheap" import.

TIP: Not sure if you are purchasing from an authorised dealer? Please contact your local state Boating Industry Association that can assist with your enquiry. You may wish to undertake a BIA 50 point Safety Check for little cost. Whilst it is not a pre-purchase appraisal, it's a great way to better understand what you are intending to purchase.

Importing A Boat

Importing a cheap boat from countries such as the USA or Asia seems to be gaining popularity. Boat buyers are talking about the "fantastic deals on offer" buying a boat from a dealer or central broker in the US. Apparently, they have access to: liquidation stock, bank and finance company repos, bankruptcies and the like. Emails are being received daily, from US dealers to buyers here in Australia with listings of boats and PWCs for sale.

All sounds familiar? Well BUYER BEWARE....There's no such thing as a FREE LUNCH, just like there is no such thing as a CHEAP BOAT!

Several of these boats have recently arrived at our service centre for what seemed like a simple annual service. Little did both of the owners know what was discovered by our senior service technician and mechanics once we connected our laptop to the engine management system for readouts (available only to authorised service centres). One was identified with cracks in the fuel-injectors and the other with water in the fuel tank and significant damage to pistons. What was a cheap boat to begin with all of a sudden has turned into a very, very expensive exercise.

Below is a list that prospective buyers, should be aware of:

1. Buy from an Accredited Dealer who is a member of the Boating Industry Association. Accredited Dealers operate business in both an ethical and professional manor, with the highest standards – in short; they are the leaders of the boating industry. An Accredited Dealer follows a set of audited guidelines, aiming to provide higher standards of excellence within the industry.
2. An Accredited Dealer will proudly display the logo to demonstrate to the purchasing public, you can buy with confidence from this dealership.
3. Specifically, Accredited Boat Dealers follow an agreed Code of Conduct, operate Trust Accounts and their business practices are audited to confirm compliance. All of these requirements are created to provide consumer protection, thus increasing buyer confidence.
4. Accredited Dealers **should** issue the buyer with a Statutory Declaration confirming, the purchased vessel and/or trailer is being sold with Clear-Title and that NO finance is owing. This protects the consumer from potential police investigations etc., because the Statutory Declaration confirms that no-one has any interest whatsoever, in the vessel and/or trailer. Sadly, the Vehicle Securities Register (VSR) does not operate nationally for vessels in Australia. Because the Hull Identification Number (HIN) is not a mandatory recording requirement at the time of registration, in some states of Australia. Just go to Vic-Roads and see for yourself!
5. Vendor Statements are available from all Victorian Accredited Dealers, confirming the vessel and/or trailers service history, accidents, modifications, insurance, registration and usage.
6. Be aware that some of the boats "For Sale in the USA" - may be stolen and consequently, they may also have been "re-birthed."

Buyer Beware

7. Many US Dealers and Brokers, are all selling the same vessel, so you can't talk to the actual vendor, be wary if you are unable to understand or validate the full service history and/or usage of the vessel and/or trailer.

8. If a mechanical inspection is offered by the US Broker, then what guarantees do you have as to the inspector's qualifications, impartiality and relations with the selling dealer! A Conflict of Interest and Commission payments are both worrying factors, there's no-way to truly validate the information you are given.

9. Trailers that aren't built to the Australian Standards in the first instance, may not able to be registered by the relevant state authorities, because they are **Not Compliant**. Therefore, they may not pass the formal inspection required for registration.

10. Consequently, it's best to stick with proven, quality and reliable products. Therefore, we recommended buying a recognised Australian branded trailer. Look at the leading manufacturers such as: MacKay, Dunbier or EasyTow to name a few.

11. Buying a vessel built to Australian Compliance and Standards means it is factory fitted with the 240v electrical system, at the time of build. If it's not, it's important to have your vessel's electrical system **fully re-wired** to suit 240v, tested and issued with an Electrical Compliance Certificate. USA built boats are wired to their standard 110v. So it's not just the power point socket that needs changing. You must also change all of the wiring, electrical looms, refrigeration, air-conditioning, chargers, shore power all other electrical equipment connected. Even some brands of TV's and navigation equipment, needs to be built to suit the Southern Hemisphere - as there is a difference in "Polarity."

12. Any conversion from 240v to 110v through the use of a transformer, inverter or adapter - simply won't work, in the long-term. They have proven in the past to be both unreliable and dangerous. The risk of fire and/or electrical shock is real. Your safety and that

Buyer Beware

of your crew and guests is YOUR responsibility! Remember, electricity and water, **Do Not Mix**!

13. Insurance companies will **Not Cover** any vessel and/or trailer that are **Not Australian Compliant**. The Electrical Compliance Certificate and Registration papers may need to be lodged.

14. Check the width of the trailer to ensure your local state Registration Compliance. Being over-width will **Not Pass** inspection. Also typically, the tow-hitch and coupling height on the trailer more than likely will need to be lowered to meet Australian Compliance. A structural engineer usually can assist.

15. Vessel and engine Manufacturers Warranties, **Do Not Apply** outside the country of the purchase. Therefore, any USA installed Engine and/or hull purchased outside the authorised dealer channel here in Australia, is **Not Covered** by either vessel and engine warranty.

16. Read information published by the Outboard Engine Distributors Association (OEDA) and The Australian Marine Engine Council Inc (AMEC) on this matter. Member companies include: Mercury, Honda, Yamaha, Suzuki, Evinrude/BRP and Mariner have all individually stated that: "Buyer Beware" and to "Exercise Extreme Caution" if you're thinking of importing your own boat, because of the lack of warranty, Non-Australian Compliance and a buyers inability to understand the usage and service history.

17. Australian Consumer and Trade Practices, Regulations and Laws, **Do Not Apply** to the selling dealers, brokers and mechanical inspectors in the USA. You have **No Legal** comeback, should you run into problems.

The bottom line, is it all worth it?

Simply, just do a deal with your local Accredited Dealer and buy an Australian Delivered and Compliant Boat at a fair and reasonable price...

Buyer Beware

After-all, the actual savings may not be as big as you think and local support, assistance and an on-going relationship will work in the long run!

Besides, buying from an Accredited Dealer means you're supporting the Australian industry which employs local people, 1000's of people in fact. Accredited Dealers and Authorised Service Centre's even offer apprenticeships and training for young men and women to learn more about the industry.

It also means that the sales and repair revenues stay here in Australia! Now that's good for us all and our economy…….

Learning from others, so you don't get it wrong!

TOP 10 mistakes other buyers have made;

Boat buyers' mistake 1: Not buying something suitable for their local conditions.

Boat buyers' mistake 2: Not doing the proper research.

Boat buyers' mistake 3: Not buying a boat from an Accredited Boat Dealer/Broker.

Boat buyers' mistake 4: Trying to do the buying exercise themselves, without the assistance of experts.

Boat buyers' mistake 5: Not understanding all of the potential costs first before buying.

Boat buyers' mistake 6: Not getting a used boat independently inspected before purchase.

Boat buyers' mistake 7: Not researching new and used boat values.

Buyer Beware

Boat buyers' mistake 8: Not buying from a local dealer by trying to import from the USA. No such thing as a free lunch.

Boat buyers' mistake 9: Not buying an Australian compliant and delivered boat or trailer through the correct channels.

Boat buyers' mistake 10: Not buying anything... Not buying a boat, just procrastinating and wasting all of that time and energy thinking about it!

10

How to SELL a boat.

Proven ways to get buyer's attention

So the time has come for you to sell your boat and depending on your motivation it could be a time of sadness, joy, relief or simple desperation. Perhaps it's just another chapter in your life is opening so it's time to move on, or time to get a bigger or smaller boat. Not forgetting there are times when your style of boating changes and buying a different boat is a real possibility that is loaded with advantages for you and your family!

Making the actual decision to sell can be rather difficult, as there are usually some pretty great memories in that boat for you, your family and friends. Your child might have caught their first fish; maybe they were standing up on water skis for the very first time…these are things I clearly remember from my first boat. I also remember mooring amongst nature in a quiet little cove having a BBQ of fresh fish that we caught at sunset. Now these are strong memories I still hold onto from my youth and my first boat.

Have a family meeting to discuss your reasons for wanting the boat sold by allowing your kids to understand the reasoning and rationale. Whatever you do, share the decision with the family, because boating is all about family after-all.

Smile, for every seller, there is a buyer - and vice versa. So let's go find the right buyer at the right price. Making the actual decision to sell can open a can of worms for those who don't have a clear understanding of expectations and the right process to do so. The first decision a seller must make is to identify who is going to sell the boat for them. The choices are usually either; tackle the sale of your boat yourself, this is called a Private Sale or hire the professional services of a *Boat Dealer/Broker.*

What's your boat worth?

Now it's time for the reality check that most sellers just don't want to acknowledge. That is; "what's my boat worth?" We are talking the actual value of the boat in today's marketplace. After all if you've made a decision to sell your boat, then the value in today's market can only be the value that a buyer would pay for it today, if it were for sale. No this is not the value that you paid for it three years ago when you purchased it, but its value now.

To achieve this value now, it's a matter of taking a step back; removing all emotional attachments to the boat, remembering that any new buyer will not place any value on the seller's emotional attachments. Usually they will compare your boat's options and accessories to whatever else is out there offered for sale.

Like most possessions we accumulate during our lifetime, the real world valuation is only confirmed when the item is actually sold. So until then, it is only a notional figure we have in our minds.

How to SELL a boat

> **TIP:** Do your research using the wonderful online resources we have available to us all and it won't cost you a cent. Compare all of the boats offered for sale both new and used on the following leading websites:
> - www.boatpoint.com.au
> - www.boatsales.com.au
> - www.boatsonsale.com.au
> - www.boatsplus.com.au
> - www.boatonline.com.au

Ensure you accurately compare; year, engine, hours, trailer, accessories, and service history. Take the time to contact a few sellers and talk with them about their boat and what price they may take if you make a cash offer. Just so you can get a direct comparison with yours, find out what the true selling price is when the vendor is squeezed, because this is never the price its advertised for.

Note exactly how many like boats are offered for sale at the moment, there is no point being priced in the middle of the road when there are 20, 30 or 50 others offered for sale as there just aren't that many buyers around. Remember all advertised prices are the prices the vendors would love to get, but this NEVER happens.

Pricing your boat correctly is absolutely critical. You may decide to price her slightly higher for a few weeks just to get a feel for the market and see whether buyers show interest in your boat. You can always reduce the price of your boat, but it is really hard to put the price up during your sales campaign, actually near on impossible. Remember in today's market, buyers have the world at their fingertips. They can even import

How to SELL a boat

a boat themselves from distressed overseas markets such as the USA and Europe.

Consequently, if you don't price your boat at the right level in the first instance, prospective buyers may choose to import a boat from overseas, so your target audience may shrink. We all know that when you buy a motor vehicle and drive it out of the dealerships showroom, she loses thousands of dollars! Well a boat is NO different, depreciation is significant, so be realistic about her true value otherwise you're only kidding yourself.

Now you have your realistic price range in your mind, it's time to test the waters and contact your preferred Accredited Dealer/Broker and ask them to value your boat. Ask them to put their valuation in writing and retain it for your files (you'll never know when you may need it). The dealer should be able to value your boat from photos you can email to them. It is not really necessary for you to drive or tow your boat to the

TIP: For example at St Kilda Boat Sales, we offer a free online service for market appraisals. You can just simply fill in the email form off our website, attach some pictures and upon receipt, we'll do the appropriate market research and within 48 hours provide you with a personalized, confidential & realistic market appraisal - at no charge, obligation free.

www.stkildaboatsales.com.au/sell-your-boat

In addition, we are an approved Club Marine Insurance Valuer, so our market appraisals are always based on facts such as recent sales of similar or like vessels, replacement values and buyer enquiry.

Dealer/Broker; digital photos (inside, outside, engine, cabins, helm etc.) should suffice.

If your boat is under finance then you need to consider exactly how much you owe. Call your finance company or lender and ask for a payout figure, they should confirm this in writing either by email or fax. You will need to understand whether you will be able to pay out the finance company in full from the sales proceeds. If you're short (i.e. finance payout is more than the actual boat's sell price or valuation), then you will need to payout the finance company in full by topping up any shortfall yourself.

The finance company will not let you sell the boat without a clear title, so you have to pay them out. Armed with the finance payout (if applicable) now you can consider all of your options, with a little more knowledge.

Private Sale

When it comes time to sell the boat, many individuals choose to handle the sale themselves; this is called a private sale. Before going down this path, make sure you are properly educated about the process and you have considered the other options available to you.

Benefits:
- More money in your own pocket (no commission or fees).
- You maintain control of the entire process.
- With proper planning and the help of this book, it will be easier to find the right buyer.

Disadvantages:
- The process of selling a boat is time consuming.
- You must educate yourself about the boat market.
- You will need to conduct your own advertising campaign.

- It's up to you to handle all of the buyer's questions and enquiries.
- You will need to complete all the sales and registration paperwork.
- You will need to learn the processes, such as sea-trials and surveys.

Advertising Advice for Private Sellers

Forget what everyone else says, you want a simple advertising campaign that is not going to cost you a fortune that gets results. Of course, everyone does!

Here are three simple steps that will get your phone ringing and emails coming:

1. Show them, what you've got for sale.
2. Tell them, what you've got for sale.
3. Tell them, where to get it.

Show Them

Clean your boat and remove everything that is not for sale and not included in the purchase price. Tidy her up and give her a good wash and a polish (if you can). Clean the covers with a pressure washer and hand wash your clears with Plexus, to remove any stains.

Take the carpets out and wash them down, let dry and place back. Clean your bilge; oil residue only infers a leaking engine.

Take her to a nice location and get plenty of photos with your digital camera, iPhone, iPad or Smartphone. Make sure your pictures are clean and not cropped; take from the outside preferably on a sunny day with blue sky behind the boat. It really shows the clean lines of a boat and after-all boating is best when it's sunny, so a sunny backdrop makes sense. Take photos of the engine(s), trailer, helm area, cabins, toilet/shower, saloon, deck, transom and cockpit. You may have 20-30 photos, keep the photos on your computer so you can easily email them to interested buyers.

Carefully select about 5-10 photos which you'll use for most of your advertising, consistency is good and makes it easy for buyers to identify if their searching through different advertising mediums. Choose a hero photo, this is the one photo of the outside of the boat that you'll use as your main photo for everything.

A few nice adverts placed into some hand-selected print and online mediums will get results, so my recommendation is for the following:

- Trailer Boat Magazine (for a Trailerable Boat)

OR

- Trade-A-Boat Magazine (for a larger Water-Based Boat)

Online with;

- Boatpoint.com.au (for all boats, regardless of the length)
- Boatsales.com.au (for all boats, regardless of the length)
- Boatsonsale.com.au (for all boats, regardless of length)
- Boatsonline.com.au (for all boats, regardless of length)
- Boatsplus.com.au (for all boats, regardless of length)

Your advertisements should be in colour only, forget black and white it looks poor and patchy at best. Remember that not every buyer has access to a computer so the internet alone is not a good idea and some buyers live in regional areas where fast internet is not available yet. So a print advertisement will ensure that every buyer has access to view your boat.

There are plenty of good websites available to get your boat to the biggest possible audience of buyers; however I'd just stick to the above listed sites, as this will cover the bulk of the marketplace on a national basis. Don't advertise into a single state, it's much cheaper to cast your net wider and to the biggest market place possible for your advertising dollars.

Tell Them What You've Got

Armed with your really good photos and your hero shot, now it's time to tell buyers some of the specifics of the boat. Write a draft and have a think before you dictate your ad wording or complete the online process. Planning really helps!

You'll need to make note of the answers to the following: make, model, year built, engine, horse power and trailer details.

Pick several features to identify, but pick only a couple of the best, as you'll have a space limitation. Don't write an essay and be specific e.g. if it's a fishing boat then say so, talk about the great fishing accessories fitted. Remember buyers will appreciate and focus on this.

Tell Them Where To Get It

Make sure your ad has your name and phone number, simple isn't it? You'd be surprised how many ads don't have contact numbers. Make sure you follow-up any calls with prompt attention. Buyers hate to wait and if you don't follow them up and return their calls a.s.a.p., then they will call other sellers and you'll miss out on the sale. Remember if you don't call back the buyers, then you may as well not have advertised in the first place.

Inspections and Sea-Trials (Private Sale)

So you've had a few calls and a buyer has made an appointment to come around and have a look. Hopefully the buyer will actually turn up;

    a) on-time

    b) on the day agreed

    c) turn up at all

How to SELL a boat

> **TIP:** Possibly the biggest area of disappointment with the private sale process is waiting for buyers who promise to come and inspect, actually turning up, especially if you're taking time off work to meet with them.
>
> If you're not prepared to wait around and have a few no-shows, then forget the private sale option and go find a boat Dealer/Broker who will do this for you.
>
> Maybe your time is better spent elsewhere, doing other things, other than trying to find a buyer for your boat.

If and when your buyers turn up, let them have a good look around the boat, answer their questions when asked, but let them spend time aboard absorbing what you're offering for sale.

The buyer may want to go for a run (actually called a sea-trial) in the boat. This is not an unreasonable request if they are a genuine buyer. However, my recommendation is NOT to take them for a sea-trial just yet, or at least until you've agreed to the money and the terms of an offer first.

Otherwise you'll take them for a run and then they will say they're not interested or offer less money than you want, so that's all a waste of time!

To satisfy the curiosity of a buyer in the first instance, you may offer to start the engine(s) with earmuffs or run the engine in a wheelie-bin full of water! If it's a water-based boat, then absolutely start the engine(s). If you don't or can't, then the buyer may think you're hiding something.

If you do take them for a sea-trial, remember it's not an afternoon cruise nor is it a fishing trip, it's a short run maybe 10-15 minutes and let the buyer take the wheel if they are licensed and your boat is insured. If not, discuss with a buyer in advance and agree on a strategy together.

No matter how good your boat is in poor conditions, it is never advisable to go for a run in unsafe boating conditions. No sale is worth that, afterall you don't want to injury your buyer or yourself, as your boat comes off a wave!! Also remember that safety gear for the sea-trial is the seller's responsibility, so ensure you are compliant.

Appoint a Boat Dealer/Broker

'Give it to the professionals'.

The boat Dealer/Broker is a trained industry professional who ideally should be a current member of the Boating Industry Association in your state. Often there is confusion surrounding the definition and role of a boat dealer vs. broker, let me explain:

- Boat Dealer is a person who: actually owns the boat which they are selling.
- Boat Broker is an: appointed sales agent who acts on behalf of a vendor (vendor agent) on a commission basis only, without having title to the property in which they are selling (aka: consignment sale)

In both description's a Dealer and a Broker is a person who acts as an intermediary between two or more parties in negotiating agreements and the like.

Like in most industries, there are dealers and there are Dealers. I believe it is really important to find a dealer who is a member of the Boating Industry Association (BIA) in your home state. The BIA has offices nationally in: Victoria, NSW, WA, SA, NT and TAS and in the sunshine state is Marine Queensland. Members of the associations are governed by a strict code of conduct and ethics to ensure a sound level of business practice.

How to SELL a boat

The attraction of the marine industry lures all types of individuals, some romanced by the notion of a quick buck playing with boats. So try to stay away from any non-industry association members, as they are not governed by any code of conduct or code of ethics, whatsoever.

The bottom line is Accredited Dealer/Brokers will deliver a much higher level of service because they use a universal and well-documented and audited process, which offers added consumer protection for buyers and sellers alike. Find an Accredited Dealer/Broker where possible, there are no additional fees or charges for doing so; it's just added peace of mind.

The Dealer acts as a vendor agent and gets paid a fee to sell a boat for a seller (vendor) in a similar role to that of a real estate agent. The boat owner (aka: seller or vendor) appoints a Dealer to be his sales agent and act on the seller's behalf within a set of guidelines or parameters, for the purpose of finding a suitable buyer.

TIP: Later on, I list the details of the Boating Industry Association in your state who will gladly recommend one of their financial boat Dealer/Broker members who will assist.

Working with an Accredited Dealer/Broker opens up a few immediate opportunities that are well-worth considering:

1. **Sell your boat to a dealer - outright.**

   This means the Dealer agrees to buy the boat from you immediately for an agreed price. The dealer will typically buy the boat from you and take a chance by putting her for sale in the open market for a higher price. This leaves the difference between the buy price and the sell price, called a retail margin. The retail margin is the reward for the Dealer who is game enough to agree to buy the boat in the first place from the seller, therefore taking a risk. Where there is risk, there is reward, if done correctly.

Benefits:
- Quick sale usually with 48 hours.
- No waiting for a dealer to find a buyer, which may take time depending on outside factors (economy, exchange rates etc.).

Disadvantages:
- Can sometimes ask for a lesser value for boat, just because the transaction is immediate.
- Dealer usually buys where he can see an opportunity for profit (maybe big or small).

2. Trade-In

If your intention is to replace your existing boat with another, maybe you're going bigger, maybe your downsizing, you may want to consider using your boat as a trade-in. As in the car industry a Dealer will offer you a value for your trade-in and you then deduct that value from the purchase price, leaving a changeover value. It's this changeover value that you need to pay and at the same time surrendering your trade-in to the boat dealer who will on-sell to another client.

Benefits:
- Quick sale and leaves you with exactly what you want,
- Removes the hassle of finding a buyer.

Disadvantages:

- Your trade-in may be worth more money to sell it to a buyer separately, but this takes time and patience.

3. Consignment / Brokerage Sale

Perhaps the most common of all the ways to sell a boat is the consignment/brokerage styled sale. This is where a success fee is paid to the seller upon finding a suitable buyer at the right price. Ultimately, the Dealer/Broker will find a buyer by undertaking an agreed advertising and marketing campaign for your boat at the agreed sell price. Once a buyer is found, the seller receives a sales commission, which is usually a percentage of the actual sell price. Also known as the fee for service or it may be a flat $ fee which is paid by the seller, out of the sales proceeds.

All other monies will be paid to the seller on the day the buyer agrees to pay for the boat in full. This is called the settlement.

Benefits:
- If your boat is at a marina, then you should be able to still use the boat whilst a buyer is being found.
- Vendors can set the agreed selling price range.
- Sales campaign can be monitored and the selling price may be reduced over the course of the sales campaign.
- Dealers will meet buyers for inspections, so the vendors don't have to worry and allocate time to the sales process.
- Hiring an industry professional to find the right buyer at the right price for your boat.
- Dealers may have buyers already registered on their books.
- Dealers don't get paid commission, until they find a buyer for your boat.

- No real downside for a seller, by using an Accredited Dealer/Broker.

Disadvantages:
- Paying a fee or sales commission to a dealer / broker for selling the boat.

Dealer/Broker - Sales Commission

I often get asked what is the standard sales commission or fee for service that is payable as a percentage of the actual sell price for using an Accredited Dealer/Broker in Australia, to sell your boat.

The table below represents the standard percentages as charged by accredited Dealers/Brokers nationally. This is a guide only and you should discuss your specific boat and the entire sales process directly with your preferred accredited Dealer/Broker as part of your intention to sell your boat.

Sell Price A$	Commission	Marketing Fee's
0 - 20,000	15% incl GST	Marketing campaign included
20,000 - 100,000	10% incl GST	Marketing campaign included
100,000 - 200,000	8% incl GST	Marketing campaign included
200,000 - 500,000	5% incl GST	Marketing campaign included
500,000 - +	by negotiation	Marketing campaign included

It is common practice to simply negotiate a flat dollar amount payable to your Accredited Dealer/Broker upon a successful sale, rather than for opting to select the percentage calculation. Maybe you decide that anything a buyer pays in excess of an agreed figure is paid to the Accredited Dealer/Broker as his commission, this is fine too.

The key to a successful sale is that you both agree on a figure. Needless to say, it is really important that the Accredited Dealer/Broker feels motivated to find the **right buyer** at the **right price**.

Preparation for Sale

Presentation is really important and this exercise should be taken as seriously as if it were your house you're putting on the market. Whoever created the expression "never judge a book by its cover" was not a boat buyer. The boat buyer will remember and be able to identify a boat by her presentation and cleanliness and so will the partner of the buyer as well. It's the first and last thing buyers look for, so it's worthwhile making a good first impression.

Remove all items that are not included with the sale.

Buyers do not like seeing messy or untidy vessels, especially those that are full of the seller's personal items. This perception makes buyer's feel like the vessel including the engine(s) has not been cared for. Experience suggests that "junk and stuff" can make your boat feel way too small.

Collate all your paperwork.

At the time of formalising your listing with your appointed Accredited Dealer/Broker you will be required to provide copies of the following:

1. You're Proof of Ownership (your original receipt of purchase).
2. Current Registration for both vessel and/or trailer.

3. Service, repair and maintenance receipts, these form the service history.
4. Owner's manual, booklets and papers.
5. Current insurance policy or current Certificate of Currency.
6. Set of engine and cabin keys.

Service your boat and/or trailer before listing her for sale.

Ensure you retain your service receipts as it offers proof and validation to the buyer that she's been cared for. Remember, a boat recently serviced removes the need of the buyer to discount your vessel even further, allowing you to stand your ground when negotiating. The less a buyer feels he needs to spend to get the boat and trailer in the right and safe condition to get onto the water now, simply means less money the buyer needs to discount, which means the more money for you!

Will she pass a pre-purchase inspection?

By undertaking a full service just before she is actually listed for sale, means that sales process will be far simpler for all. Because when your Accredited Dealer/Broker recommends to genuine buyers to make a formal offer subject to a satisfactory sea-trial and pre-purchase inspection, you know your boat and trailer will easily pass the test. You'd be surprised at how many boats listed for sale don't pass inspections, which becomes a waste of time for the buyers, sellers and Dealer/Brokers alike.

The Dealer/Broker recommendation of a formal pre-purchase inspection during the sales process is a positive approach towards closing the sale. Especially given that there is no legal or statutory requirement upon a Dealer/Broker to offer warranty of any kind whatsoever. Consequently, the pre-purchase inspection is a very good thing because;

- It ensures that buyers understand exactly what they are buying, so no surprises later.

How to SELL a boat

- Safeguards buyers purchase a boat that is fit for purpose and will be safe if operated and maintained in accordance with manufacturer's instructions.
- Protects both the Vendor and Accredited Dealer/Broker after the purchase.

So now you understand why a mechanical inspection is so important and sellers should see this as a positive process which creates a win/win for everyone.

This is a good thing because you won't have to deal with buyers who are unhappy with their purchase and any item that is not fixed or repaired will usually be identified in the pre-purchase inspection. As this inspection is paid-for by the buyer, everything that is wrong with the vessel (regardless of the seller's disclosure) will get questioned, checked and tested.

TIP: Sellers please do not hide information; your honest disclosure is appreciated. If you have or know of a problem with your boat, please tell the boat Dealer/Broker and a strategy can be discussed to address this issue. After all, the lives of your buyers may depend on it. Besides, it will be cheaper for you in the long run. Remember that buyers are not silly; they are educated better than ever before. They pay good money for a pre-purchase inspection and given their inspectors are getting paid to find problems and uncover issues, nothing ever goes unreported or slips-through, so your honest disclosure saves everyone's time and credibility in the long run.

The Law Of Reciprocity

'Do unto others, as you would like done to you'. I like to call it the 'Karma Train'. Remember what goes around comes around.

Engagement Of A Dealer/Broker

To begin the sales process, of finding a buyer, your accredited dealer/broker will require you to sign an Engagement of Agent document that is applicable to all brokerage and/or consignment sales.

Additionally, to comply with dealer accreditation requirements for the Boating Industry Association in some states - all vendors will need to complete and sign a Vendor Statement. The purpose of these documents is to confirm:

1. Your ownership of the actual vessel and/or trailer.
2. The appointment of the accredited dealer/broker to sell your vessel and on what basis. i.e. duration of appointment and exclusivity of listing.
3. The fee for service (sales commission) which is payable by the seller to the accredited dealer upon successful sale.
4. Confirmation of whether or not the vessel is under finance and is to be supported by a statutory declaration.
5. The agreed "sell price range" outlining high and low ranges and parameters of the price range.
6. Outlines ALL fees and charges for the marketing and advertising of your vessel to the wider marketplace as part of the agreed sales campaign.
7. Statement of purpose for which the vendor has been using the vessel.
8. Basic information in relation to the vendor's experience of using the boat. This will be passed onto the buyer at settlement.

All documents MUST only be completed and signed by the actual vessel owner(s) or by appointed representative (under Power Of Attorney). These will also be co-signed by a representative of the Accredited Dealer/Broker and both parties for future reference should retain copies.

Selling With Clear-Title

Before the sales process begins, your Accredited Dealer/Broker will ask you for full disclosure of any finance agreements in place applicable to your ownership of the boat and trailer. That means have you borrowed any money or have lien to buy the boat and trailer? (E.g. bank, lender, finance company, business or an individual).

Vehicle Securities Register (VSR)

The Vehicle Securities Register is a national register of encumbered vehicles which includes the records of: motor cars, motor cycles and trailers, but sadly doesn't always include vessels (boats). The VSR records the Vehicle Identification Number (VIN) on a central and national database managed by all of the motor registration authorities in each state of Australia. The VSR records whether a financial institution has a financial interest or moneys owning on the item. So if you don't payout that item in full to the finance company when sold, the item cannot be resold with clear title. Not only is this against the law.... but it will be repossessed at any time if those moneys with interest, are not paid in full. So the last thing you want is your boat and trailer being repossessed because of the lack of disclosure by the previous owner.

Whilst a lot of behind the scenes work by the state Registration Authorities and Boating Industry Associations nationally is being undertaken to resolve this issue, it is still not a mandatory requirement for the **H**ull **I**dentification **N**umber (HIN) to be recorded as part of the registration process, therefore the VSR is not really a neither true nor accurate check.

To overcome the VSR issue, your Accredited Dealer/Broker will ask for a Statutory Declaration to be signed and witnessed by a suitably qualified

How to SELL a boat

person. This will be handed over at settlement to the buyer to state the boat and trailer are being sold with clear title.

A Statutory Declaration is a written statement declared to be true in the presence of an authorised witness. A person wishing to use a statutory declaration in connection with a law of the Commonwealth, the Australian Capital Territory or certain other Territories must make the declaration in accordance with the Statutory Declarations Act 1959 (the Act) and the Statutory Declarations Regulations 1993 (the Regulations).

Under the act a person who willfully makes a false statement in a statutory declaration is guilty of an offence and may be fined or jailed, or both.

The act provides that a Statutory Declaration must be in the prescribed form and must be made before a prescribed witness. The form for making a statutory declaration and the persons who can witness a Statutory Declaration are prescribed under the regulations.

TIP: A sample Statutory Declaration and listing of appropriate witnesses, is available towards the back of this book for your use.

Monies Owing (Buying With Clear Title)

Should your boat and trailer have monies owing to any 3rd party, your Accredited Dealer/Broker will ask for a written confirmation of the payout figures plus all contract numbers and banking details from your financier or lender. It is your Accredited Dealer/Broker's role to ensure and process all payments to interested parties and finance companies on behalf of the seller. This means that all interested parties are paid out (in full) at the time of settlement, so no one has to worry or be concerned in the future.

Settlements will not take place until the finance company has provided written confirmation of the payout. In the event of a shortfall or deficit, the boat or trailer owner is solely responsible to pay the difference before settlement. Otherwise, the finance company or lender will not issue clear title and the sale cannot proceed. Likewise any surplus funds at settlement will be credited to the lawful vessel owner.

The payout details and payment receipts will be recorded and at settlement your Accredited Dealer/Broker must issue you with a formal letter, remittance advice or statement; showing all deductions, finance company payments and the net payment for your files. Receipts for all finance company payments should be included for easy reference.

Smartphones

Your industry Accredited Dealer/Broker will be aware of the new and evolving technologies such as iPhone, iPad, Blackberry, and Google Android. This technology offers immediate access to tech savvy buyers and must be considered in today's electronic world.

Ask your Accredited Dealer/Broker to outline to you how they communicate with registered buyers via text messages, notifications and ask if they have an App (for iPhone & iPad) available for download from iTunes or an Android App available for download from Google Play.

How to SELL a boat

Given that these technology-based services shouldn't cost a seller any more in terms of fees or commission, consider finding a dealer who has this in place now. Ask for a demonstration of how they can get the message about "your terrific boat and trailer being offered for sale" and how buyers should consider an inspection, before buying another boat!

It's not hard to get a message out to buyers on a national basis, remember all your Accredited Dealer/Broker needs to do is find the **right buyer** at the **right price**, after all how hard can that be?

TIP: Download our "Boat Sales" App on Android or iPhone/iPad from iTunes. For iPhone/iPad users you will be able to receive free text messages called notifications. The benefit is that whenever we list a new boat for sale or reduce the price of an existing boat, buyers will be informed immediately by free text message. After-all we live in the communication age.

By simply turning on notifications, interested parties will get the information before others and before our other advertising hits the streets. You will also get reminders for events like daylight savings, boat shows and the like.

Unrelated but a free plug: Also with our "Boat Sales" App you will be able to view <live> our Web Cam from the top of the lighthouse at St Kilda Marina. So you can check the conditions **before** you go boating! (In-App purchase, a small one-time fee applies)

>  **TIP:** Here's the link to our App on Apple iTunes:
> http://ax.itunes.apple.com/au/app/boat-sales/id386136164?mt=8#ls=1
> Or follow the links from: www.stkildaboatsales.com.au

Typical sales campaign

The following elements maybe used in a national campaign undertaken by your Accredited Dealer/Broker:

- **Magazine Advertising**
  a. Trade-A-Boat Magazine and/or
  b. Trader Boat Magazine

- **Internet Advertising**
  a. The Accredited Dealers website
  b. BoatPoint.com.au
  c. BoatSales.com.au
  d. Boatsonsale.com.au
  e. Boatsplus.com.au
  f. Yachthub.com.au
  g. Boatsonline.com.au

- **Social media sites**
  Including: Twitter, Facebook, Linked-In and YouTube

- **Detailed Vessel Inventory**

A4 colour brochure includes: digital photos and lists technical specifications, engine & registration details, options and accessories:

- For sale board affixed to your boat. Optional and removable.
- Free storage for boat and trailer whilst advertised for sale.
- Contract preparation, negotiation and execution.
- Registration transfers to be lodged on behalf of the buyer and the seller.

Receiving An Offer

There are many differing descriptions of the term offer and it does depend on what you are selling. I really like this description found on the website: *www.businessdictionary.com*

"Voluntary, but conditional promise submitted by a buyer or seller (offeror) to another (offeree) for acceptance, and which becomes legally enforceable if accepted by the offeree".

"An offer (unlike a solicitation) is a clear indication of the offeror's willingness to enter into an agreement under specified terms, and is made in a manner that a reasonable person would understand its acceptance will result in a binding contract".

Offers normally include a closing date, otherwise a period of 14 days after the date of offer is commonly assumed. Terms and conditions under which an offer is made are:

- Price
- Delivery date
- "Subject To" (special conditions)

How to SELL a boat

o   Finance.

o   Satisfactory pre-purchase inspection by a qualified person at the buyer's expense on/or before.

o   Satisfactory hull inspection by a qualified person at the buyer's expense on/or before….

o   Satisfactory sea-trial.

o   Validation of service history.

o   Marina berth or storage allocation/availability at buyer's expense.

So in terms of locking down a buyer, your accredited dealer/broker should ask a buyer to make a formal offer for submission to the vendor (ideally in writing) which confirms they follow:

• Price to be paid.

• Deposit payment which must be held in a trust styled account until settlement.

• Settlement & hand over (date when final monies to be paid).

• "Subject To"

Typically your Accredited Dealer/Broker will call the vendor (or forward email) to advise them of the offer. The next steps would be either:

• The Dealer/Broker will discuss the offer in detail.

• Make a recommendation to the vendor, outlining what strategy to adopt, which will be based on overall buyer interest for the boat during the sales campaign.

- Await the vendor's instructions, who can either:
    a. Accept the offer.
    b. Ask for more money.
    c. Decline the offer and explain why.

To most experienced boat Accredited Dealer/Brokers, offers are not real offers if they do not answer the above questions, because once the vendor agrees, buyers are expected to sign contracts and pay deposits without hesitation, further negotiation and without fuss. Anything less than an offer, means your buyer is not really ready to buy and is just checking out an Accredited Dealer/Broker and vendor, which is a waste of everyone's time.

Pre-Purchase Inspection

Most buyers in today's market will want an independent pre-purchase inspection to uncover and eliminate any potential surprises with their boat purchase. Most will want to find out the exact condition before they commit. Given that some used boat purchases are not covered by dealer warranty and knowing that it's not a legal requirement for Accredited Dealer/Broker to offer any warranty with a used boat purchase, it is advisable and recommended that all advertised particulars and information about the boat is designed to be a guide only and all buyers are strongly advised to hire the professional services of a qualified marine surveyor and/or mechanic, during the purchase process and to thoroughly check the particulars and safe vessel operation.

The purchaser should inspect the vessel and/or trailer to satisfy them as to its sea and/or roadworthiness, condition, specification and Australian Builders Plate (ABP) compliance.

 **TIP:** For vessels that are over 15-years-old and/or powered by petrol carburetor engines a mechanical inspection should be mandatory.

To find a suitably qualified, independent marine professional to undertake your inspection, please contact the Boating Industry Association in your state or ask your selling Accredited Dealer/Broker who should be able to recommend a few a suitable persons.

Any Dealer/Broker who has a service, workshop or repair facilities, should not offer to undertake an inspection as this may be considered a conflict of interest and after all is not really independent. Also a Dealer/broker should not receive any form of payment, commission or reward whatsoever, for recommending a particular inspection person or company, as published in the Boating Industry Association Code of Ethics and Code of Conduct.

Results of Inspection

So the independent pre-purchase inspection has been carried out at the buyer's expense, where to from here? Depending on the results of the inspection, below is the suggested course of action:

Pass – No faults or problems

Terrific, agree on a settlement date and start completing registration transfers for both boat and trailer in readiness for settlement. Also prepare a Statutory Declaration and ensure a suitably qualified person signs as a witness to the vendor's signature.

> **TIP:** Have the buyer email you or ask to countersign the purchase papers to confirm that he is satisfied with the test and agrees to buy unconditionally.

Pass – But things report as faulty

Obtain a copy of the inspection report for your file and have a good read. Ask the buyer what they plan to do. This typically depends on the level and significance of the faulty items as to whether or not they still want to proceed with the sale.

Try to gain an idea from a qualified marine mechanic as to the actual cost of the repairs of the faulty items. It is much better than speculating or listening to the buyer. Some buyers may see this as an opportunity to use this as a tool for gaining additional discount off the purchase price. Perhaps with good reason, but also because they know they can get the faults repaired at half the price of what is being discussed!

Usually cool heads with open dialogue outlining the actual cost of repairs and or the significance of the damaged items may help each party to better understand each other's situation.

In a perfect world, each party agrees to split the costs of repairs and therefore the sale is confirmed.

Sometimes you can't agree to work this out to every one's satisfaction; therefore you don't really have any other choice, but to refund the buyer's deposit.

How to SELL a boat

> **TIP:** Record on the purchase documents whatever agreement was made with the buyer. Ask your buyer to email you or ask them to countersign the purchase papers to confirm that he is now satisfied with the test and agrees to buy unconditionally.

Fail Test – Worst Case:

This is a really tough and difficult area to try and solve, but ultimately the boat failed its test and the reasons are now formally documented on the report and the buyer scared off. You don't really have any other choice, but to refund the buyers deposit.

Afterwards, have a read of the report and as the vendor you should pay for all of the noted repairs and faults to simply get her right - for the next buyer. Ultimately, if this cannot be achieved, you may not find a buyer at all. Consequently, you may wish to withdraw her from the market.

Alternatively, reduce the price to a point where buyers are happy to buy on an as is basis meaning a buyer has waived his right to a pre-purchase inspection and ensure that when she is sold, you note this on the contract so there is no recourse later on and your arse is covered!

> **TIP:** Remember before when I outlined the importance of getting the boat and trailer serviced before listing her for sale? Well if you would have correctly done that before, then you wouldn't be losing a buyer and refunding a deposit. Remember, everything comes out in the open when your boat is inspected at the request of a buyer.

Honey, let's buy a BOAT!

Deposit Payments

When selling your boat ensure the buyer leaves a decent deposit. The deposit is required by law to complete one of the legal requirements for a contract to be activated.

A decent deposit is usually (10%) of the purchase price, which is not essential, but preferred. I recommend that a deposit be any amount that is enough to make an impact on the buyer, so they will think twice about losing the money if they pull out of the sale.

An Accredited Dealer/Broker must hold the deposit monies in a trust styled account, which is a legal requirement until the purchase is paid in full and all monies are released. Tax Invoices and receipts will be issued.

Settlement and Handover

Given that most of us bank online, settlement will usually be carried out when your buyer pays for the boat in full.

Bank or personal cheques are not usually accepted as final payment unless the boat dealer/broker or private seller knows you personally. Sadly, these can all be cancelled and don't clear when deposited into your account for 3-5 days, so it is not advisable to release your boat until those funds are cleared and verified by your bank. Internet or bank transfers are the best method and can be arranged between banks usually for a fee, so ask your personal or business banker to assist.

Sales going through an Accredited Dealer/Broker will not release the boat to the buyer until those funds are verified as received. Remember to ensure that there are no monies owing by the seller for a finance company, lender or the like. So get your statutory declaration signed by the seller and hand to the buyer at settlement, make a copy for your files.

Handover is when the boat keys are given to the buyer at which time you should go through the operation of the boat with the buyer. Show him where the battery switches are located and give a good overview, as your buyer's safety and enjoyment will largely depend on the detail you can give.

Vendor Payments At Settlement

At settlement your Accredited Dealer/Broker should be able to transfer your sales process to your nominated account. The funds you will receive should be of no surprise if you know the actual agreed selling price discussed with you during the negotiation process.

Your engagement of agent document that you signed to appoint the Accredited Dealer/Broker in the first place, will have the commission payable listed, so just deduct one from the other.

Any other deductions made by the Accredited Dealer/Broker at settlement should have been discussed with you prior. Items like: finance company payouts, boat washing, sales video production, mechanical repairs need to have supporting documentation (invoice) to accompany them.

After the settlement your Accredited Dealer/Broker must issue you with a formal letter, remittance advice or statement showing all deductions and the net payment to you for your files.

11

Safety and Weather Briefing

You're the Skipper, You're Responsible

Carrying the required safety equipment in good working order is essential for your safety on the water and depending on your boating location it may also be a legal requirement. Proven many times over in emergency situations, having immediate access to good-quality and well-maintained safety equipment does in fact save lives. Remember, as a boat owner and/or the skipper, the safety of you, your crew and passengers depends on it.

Some of the information provided below, together with images, diagrams and advice used throughout this chapter on safety and weather have been reprinted with permission and is used under Licence from: Transport Safety Victoria (TSV) whose support for this book has been tremendous and greatly appreciated.

For more information, please visit: www.transportsafety.vic.gov.au

Check your local authority

 TIP: It is very strongly recommended to check with your local marine safety organisation and the Weather Bureau in your region, before you go boating.

Seek current information on local conditions and the required safety equipment before you depart. You must also prepare your boat and passengers according to the weather and situations you may encounter. The safety of you and your family depend on it.

Remember as Maritime NSW accurately reminds us all:

"You're the Skipper, You're Responsible."

Requirements for safety equipment vary; based on the type of vessel you are operating, the waterway and Australian state you are operating it in and in some cases, your distance from the shoreline. I also suggest you check with your local state based authority as to the requirements for safety before you go boating.

Below is a listing of your local authority for your convenience:

Safety and Weather Briefing

Who is your local boating authority responsible for safety regulations?

New South Wales & ACT
Maritime NSW Ph: 13 12 56
www.maritime.nsw.gov.au

Northern Territory
Northern Territory Transport Group Ph: 1300 654 628
www.transport.nt.gov.au/safety/marine

Queensland
Maritime Safety Queensland Ph: 07) 3120 7462
www.msq.qld.gov.au

South Australia
Department Transport, Energy Infrastructure Ph: 13 10 84
www.sa.gov.au

Tasmania
Marine & Safety Tasmania Ph: 1300 135 513
www.mast.tas.gov.au

Victoria
Transport Safety Victoria Ph: 1800 223 022
www.transportsafety.vic.gov.au
(formerly: Marine Safety Victoria)

Western Australia
Department of Transport Ph: 1300 362 416
www.transport.wa.gov.au

Weather and Tides

Weather is one of the greatest boating hazards. Accessing current weather information, understanding it properly, and knowing how it will affect where you are boating is essential.

Before you go out on the water, always check the weather using a marine weather forecast. Land and general forecasts do not take into account wind-speed over water, which is double that over land.

If you intend to be away for a day or two, obtain a long-range weather forecast. The weather can change suddenly and without warning.

While marine forecasts are almost always accurate when predicting major weather events, such as gales, they can be less accurate when predicting local changes of conditions.

Where can I check weather and tidal conditions?

The Bureau of Meteorology (BOM) provides all the latest information required by boaters including weather conditions, tidal conditions and wind warnings.

Visit: *www.bom.gov.au*

BOM provides reports of:
- Australian coastal water zones.
- Marine wind warnings highlighting the most extreme conditions expected in each coastal or local waters area for a following 24-hour period.
- Separate forecast and warning services for local waters such as Port Phillip, Sydney Harbour, Moreton Bay and Rottnest Island.

Marine weather warnings

Marine weather warnings are issued by BOM. Any active warnings should be taken into account before embarking on a trip.

In some states, occupants of vessels greater than 4.8m in length and up to and including 12m in length are required to wear a PFD when operating in an area where BOM has issued a current:
- Gale warning.
- Storm warning.
- Severe thunderstorm warning.
- Severe weather warning.

Weather information and Webcams

A growing number of businesses, clubs and organisations have wonderful websites that provide access to webcams and weather information freely to the boating public.

TIP: Make yourself a list of the local sites in your boating area that offer such services, even save them as a favourite or homepage on your internet browser.

Many such sites are operated by boating clubs and marinas, for example in Melbourne we own and operate the web cam situated on-top of the lighthouse at St Kilda Marina. This webcam is accessed by over 60,000 people per year and offers wonderful live images of the boating activity at the top end of Port Phillip Bay.

Webcams provide a great way to check the actual conditions before you go boating. www.stkildaboatsales.com.au/webcam.

Safety Hints and the weather
- Know the local factors that influence sea conditions and know where to reach shelter quickly.

Safety and Weather Briefing

- Learn how to read the weather map.
- Be aware that the weather map in the morning newspaper was most likely prepared the day before.
- Always check the latest forecast and warnings before going to sea and know what conditions exceed your safety limits.
- Beware of rapidly darkening and lowering clouds - squalls may be imminent.
- When at sea, listen to the weather reports on public or marine radio provided by the bureau, your state/territory marine safety agency or Volunteer Coast Radio Stations.
- Be flexible - change your plans if necessary.

Safety Equipment

Requirements for safety equipment vary based on the type of vessel you are operating, the waterway you are operating on, and in some cases, your proximity to the shore. You should familiarise yourself with the requirements for your circumstances.

Be familiar with how to operate your safety equipment, as in an emergency situation you may not have time to read the instructions. Let everyone on-board know what safety equipment is carried, where it is stored and how it works.

Equipment, Placement and Maintenance

All safety equipment required to be carried on board must be:
- Placed or located in a conspicuous and readily accessible position at all times.
- Kept in good order at all times.
- Maintained or serviced in a way that ensures they are able to be operated at all times.
- Serviced on or before the date specified by the manufacturer for that item of equipment.

Safety and Weather Briefing

- In the case of fire extinguishers, maintained in accordance with the relevant standard for fire protection equipment.

What do I need to know about my equipment?

Personal Flotation Devices (PFDs) or lifejackets

- One for each person on-board or being towed.
- Should be snug, but a comfortable fit.
- Must be the type of PFD appropriate for the:
  o Vessel type
  o Activity
  o Area of operation
  o Conditions

Fire extinguisher (powered recreational vessel)

- Dry chemical powder extinguisher required.
- Number and capacity depend on amount of fuel being carried.
- Ensure that extinguisher is charged and the needle is in the green.

Bucket with lanyard (can also double as a bailer)

- Large capacity bucket recommended.
- Ensure bucket suits shape of hull eg. Square bucket for flat floors.
- Lanyard must be attached and appropriate to the size of vessel.

Lifebuoy

- One required if vessel is more than 8 metres, but not more than 12 metres in length.
- Two required if vessel is more than 12 metres in length.

Waterproof buoyant torch

Must:

- Be operational.

Safety and Weather Briefing

- Be fully waterproof.
- Float.
- Carrying spare globes and batteries are recommended.

Bilge pumping system
- Required when vessel has covered bilge or closed underfloor compartments.
- May be electric or manual system.

Bailer
- Required when no manual or electric bilge pumping system is present.
- Large capacity bailer recommended.

Anchor and chain or line, or both
- Must be appropriate for area of operation and size of vessel.
- Several different anchor types available.
- Different anchors are used for different seabeds e.g. mud, sand, rock.

Pair of oars with rowlocks or paddles
- Required if vessel is up to and including 4.8m in length
- A spare paddle is required on-board kayaks, canoe, or raft.
- Rowing boat if travelling more than 2nm from shore on coastal waters.

Dinghy or Liferaft
- Required if vessel is more than 12 metres in length.

Hand held orange smoke signals
- Primarily for daytime use.
- Store in a waterproof container.
- Replace when expired.

Hand held red distress flares
- Primarily for night time use.
- Store in a waterproof container.
- Replace when expired.

Marine Radio
- VHF, HF or 27MHz
  o If VHF, a licence maybe required.
- Radio range varies depending on type of set installed.
- Weather and navigation warnings are available at specific times throughout the day.
- Radio is the most efficient form of remote communication.

Red star parachute distress rocket
- Fires a single star light to a height of approximately 300m.
- Keep flares away from fuels and combustibles.
- Store in a waterproof container in a readily accessible position.
- Flares should be fired when you think you are likely to be seen by someone able to assist.

Approved Emergency Position Indicating Radio Beacon (EPIRB)
- 406Mhz Digital EPIRBS have been required since 2009.
- EPIRBS must be registered with the Australian Maritime Safety Authority (AMSA).
- Registration is free.
- EPIRBS can be GPS or non GPS enhanced.
- EPIRBS with GPS enhancement reduces the search area dramatically.

Safety and Weather Briefing

Compass

- The most reliable form of direction finding when out of sight of visual reference to the coast or landmarks.
- Can include electronic or wrist mounted models (e.g. GPS, chart plotter, iPhone or iPad).

The carrying safety equipment is no substitute for proper preparation. Always conduct a check of your safety equipment as a part of your trip planning.

Depending on your state, boating location, type of boat and planned voyage, let's take a look at the different items that should be carried on-board as safety equipment.

Emergency Position Indicating Radio Beacons (EPIRB)

An Emergency Position Indicating Radio Beacon or EPIRB is a small electronic device that, when activated, assists rescue authorities to locate those in distress.

In some states all recreational vessels heading out more than two nautical miles from the coast are required to carry an approved 406 Mhz EPIRB. However, it is recommended that all vessels venturing into coastal waters carry one.

Only marine EPIRBs are accepted as safety equipment. These are designed to float in the water to optimise the signal to the satellite. Emergency Locator Transmitters (ELT) used in aircraft or Personal Locator Beacons (PLB) such as those used by bushwalkers, four-wheel drivers, other adventurers on land, employees working in remote areas, crew in boats and aircrew, are not accepted as suitable safety equipment for ships and boats.

Registering your EPIRB

You must register your EPRIB with the Australian Maritime Safety Authority (AMSA). A registered 406 MHz beacon will allow the AMSA rescue centre to find nominated emergency contacts that may be able to provide valuable information to assist with a rescue.

Registration is free and valid for two years. More details about how to register your EPIRB can be found on the AMSA website.

Flares

When operating on coastal and enclosed waters, most recreational vessels are required to carry two hand-held red distress flares and two hand-held orange smoke signals of an approved type.

Red distress flares have a visibility range of 10 km and are designed for use at night, but can also be seen during the day.

Orange smoke signals can be seen for up to 4 km (10 km by aircraft) and should be used in daylight to pinpoint your position.

A ***red star parachute distress rocket*** is required on board if vessels are travelling greater than 2 nm from the coast. They are designed to fire a single red star to a height of approximately 300 m. The star burns while falling for at least 40 seconds and can be seen from the greatest distance due to its intensity and elevation from sea level.

Flares must be stored in a cool, dry place. It is a good idea to store them in an approved waterproof flare container. These containers will also float if dropped in the water.

Operating a flare

- Read the instructions on the side of the flare.
- Make sure the wind is behind you.
- Firmly hold the flare by the yellow handle and hold the flare over the side of the boat. Caution: the metal canister burns hot so DO NOT hold the flare anywhere else.
- Unscrew the lid on the top of the flare.
- Hold the flare away from you at all times.
- Never look into the top of the flare.
- With your other hand, pull the yellow tag away from you and let the tag go.
- The flare may take several seconds to activate.
- Once the flare is activated, hold in the air, make sure wind is behind you.
- When smoke or flame has finished, drop used flare canister in the water. Do not drop the used canister in the bottom of the boat, it could burn through your hull or start a fire.

Important points to remember

- Always delay using flares until you can see an aircraft, or until people on shore or in other boats are in visual range.
- Keep flares away from fuel or combustibles and store in an accessible dry place.
- Be prepared - ensure everyone on board your vessel knows where the flares are stored and how to use them.
- Ensure that you carefully follow the activation instructions of all flares.

Flares hold a serviceable life of three years. You must ensure the flares are current and obtain new ones if their use-by-dates are reached. Expiry dates are stamped on the side of each flare.

Safety and Weather Briefing

> **TIP:** Expired out of date flares can be disposed of at some police stations and marine clubs, so please check with your local state authority. Please do not dispose of them in your rubbish bins as some rubbish particularly in regional areas may be burnt and we don't want your flare exploding, it is very dangerous. Flares ignited at sporting events are a very dangerous activity, so proper disposal is in the interests of the community! Please be aware.

Marine Radio and Communications

Distress monitoring:

What HF distress monitoring services are provided?

Marine radio distress monitoring services are provided in most boating locations along the coast and inland locations of Australia on HF frequencies 4125 kHz, 6215 kHz and 8291 kHz.

Distress frequencies are monitored by Water Police and Australian Volunteer Coast Guard Radio Communications Officers. Complementary services operate around Australia in a network of stations including: Queensland, Western Australia, New South Wales, Victoria, Tasmania and South Australia.

What VHF distress monitoring services are provided?

The Water Police and Coast guard flotilla provides distress monitoring on VHF Channel 16.

For the latest VHF information including correct frequencies and pro-

Honey, let's buy a BOAT! 247

tocols, visit the Australian Communications and Media Authority and Australian Maritime Safety Authority websites.

General information

Can I call to record my position?

Some Coast Guard flotillas will record vessel position; however, vessel operators should note the service does not provide follow-up or exception reporting.

If you are going offshore, you should always make arrangements for someone on shore to notify the relevant authorities if you don't arrive at your destination as planned. It is also recommended that arrangements be made with an appropriate communications service provider regarding vessel tracking and to monitor voyage progress.

What about navigation warnings?

Navigation warnings are broadcast on HF frequency 8176 kHz.

For example in some locations Coast Guard Radio broadcasts navigation Warnings at 07:57 and 12:57 Eastern Standard Time. Consistent with HF broadcast characteristics, not all transmissions will be received by all vessels in all locations.

Navigation warnings for local waters are broadcast on VHF channel 67. These broadcasts follow the weather.

Weather services:

How do I receive weather broadcasts with my HF radio?

Weather in Eastern Australia is broadcast on HF frequency bands 2, 6, 8 and 12 MHz at night (1800 to 0700 EST), and 4, 8, 12 and 16 MHz during the day (0700 to 1800 EST). Specifically, the Bureau of Meteorology will broadcast weather on frequencies:

Safety and Weather Briefing

- 2201 kHz, 6507 kHz, 8176 and 12365 kHz by night, and
- 4426 kHz, 8176 kHz, 12365 kHz and 16546 kHz by day.

When can I listen to the weather on HF?

Information about weather broadcast times on HF is provided by the Bureau of Meteorology.

How do I receive weather broadcasts with my VHF radio?

Weather can be heard on VHF Channel 67 by vessels in and around your local waterway. Please ask a local boater or Coast Guard for advice.

When can I listen to the weather on VHF?

VHF weather broadcast on Channel 67 for vessels in and around some waterways, and are at set times during the day.

What about other weather services?

Further information about VHF weather services around Australia is provided by Bureau of Meteorology, please check with them for your local availability.

Personal Flotation Devices (PFD)

Each state of Australia has requirements for wearing PFDs at certain times on recreational vessels. For example in Victoria, all occupants of the following vessels are required to wear a specified personal flotation device (PFD) when in an open area of the vessel that is underway:

- Powerboat up to and including 4.8metres in length.
- Off-the-beach sailing yachts.
- Personal watercraft.

Safety and Weather Briefing

- Canoes, kayaks, rowing boats and rafts.
- Pedal boats and fun boats.
- Kite boards and sail boards.
- Recreational tenders.

All occupants of the following vessels are required to wear a specified PFD at times of heightened risk when in an open area of the vessel that is underway:

- Yachts (including mono hull, trailerable and multi hull yachts, excluding off-the-beach sailing yachts).
- Powerboats greater than 4.8 m up to and including 12 m in length.

PFDs on children

Children under the age of 10 must wear a specified PFD at all times on any vessel, regardless of size, when they are in an open area of the vessel that is underway.

When choosing a PFD for a child, care should be taken to ensure that the child does not slip out of the PFD when placed in the water. This can be done by making sure that the garment fits the child and has a crotch strap. Also note that there is no current Australian standard for the manufacture of a PFD to fit a child that weighs less than 10 kilograms.

Are there different types of PFDs?

There are several different types of PFD, with varying levels of buoyancy. PFD types 1, 2 and 3 are personal flotation devices that comply with the requirements of the Marine Regulations 2009 (Vic) (Marine Regulations 2009).

- A PFD type 1 is a recognised lifejacket and will provide a high level of buoyancy and should keep the wearer in a safe floating position. They are made in high visibility colours with retro-reflective patches.

- A PFD type 2 is a buoyancy vest – not a lifejacket. It will provide less buoyancy than a PFD type 1 but should be sufficient to keep your head above water. Like a PFD Type 1, they are manufactured in high visibility colours.
- A PFD type 3 is a buoyancy garment – not a lifejacket. They have similar buoyancy to a PFD type 2 and are manufactured in a wide variety of colours.

Safety equipment for human powered vessels

The safety equipment factsheet will contain a table of the minimum safety equipment for recreational vessels of this type.

Ask your local state safety authority for a current listing of what is required.

Safety equipment for powered vessels

The safety equipment factsheet will contain a table of the minimum safety equipment for recreational vessels of this type.

> **TIP:** Remember, the responsibility for carrying accurate safety equipment for your boat is the responsibility of the skipper, which may or may not be the boat's registered owner at the time of use.

Ask your local state safety authority or Accredited Dealer/Broker for a current listing of what is required.

Safety equipment for personal watercrafts (PWC)

The safety equipment factsheet will contain a table of the minimum safety equipment for recreational vessels of this type.

Ask your local state safety authority or Accredited Dealer/Broker for a current listing of what is required.

Safe Operation

The following list is an overview of recreational boating safety guidance available on the Transport Safety Victoria (TSV) website. The information is provided to help keep you and your passengers' safe on the water and ensure the safety of those around you. You can also access key information about vessel maintenance and safety equipment.

Vessel Maintenance

You've hopefully already read my earlier chapter about the cost of boating, which outlines in detail required boat maintenance and repairs.

Vessel maintenance doesn't have to be a chore: get into a routine and maintain your boat to prevent breakdown on the water.

The four main areas to check are your:
- Motor
- Fuel
- Batteries
- Boat structure

Motor

Manufacturers usually recommend a service by a specialised workshop at least once a year- even if the motor is hardly used. This ensures vital internal parts such as the water pump are checked. If your motor is used regularly, you should change your gear-box oil every three months.

- Replace your pull cord if it is fraying.
- Check all wiring.
- Clean spark-plugs, check gaps and replace if required.
- Check compression.
- Lubricate all moving parts.
- Check and re-fill gear case oil.
- Clean cooling system passages.
- Check propeller and nut – sand or file any small cracks.
- Check and replace the sacrificial anode if required.

Fuel

- Always replace old fuel - never go out with fuel which is more than six months old.
- Make sure you have enough fuel for the trip - 1/3 out, 1/3 back and 1/3 in reserve.
- Clean your fuel tank at least once a year with a suitable solvent and dispose of old fuel responsibly.
- Inspect the fuel tank for cracks or corrosion.
- Always replace old fuel after periods of inactivity.
- Inspect fuel lines, manual priming bulb and connections for cracks and leaks.
- Clean out or replace fuel filter.
- For fuel disposal please make contact with your local council for details.

Batteries

- Top-up battery cells with distilled water and check each cell with a hydrometer.

Safety and Weather Briefing

- The battery should be charged at a rate that is suitable to the battery and should never be over-charged.
- Batteries should be secured in brackets.
- Battery terminals, cables and casing should be kept clean.
- Grease terminals regularly.
- Test all equipment that uses the battery.

Boat structure

- Clean and paint your boat regularly.
- Inspect boat for corrosion and cracks.
- Ensure all bungs are suitable and in good condition.
- Check for water and fuel leaks.
- Check and grease drain flaps.
- Ensure bilges are clean and dry.
- Test steering for stiffness - oil cables with the correct lubricant.

Transport Safety Victoria (TSV) also recommends keeping the following items on board:

- Engine manual.
- Flywheel pull rope.
- Spare 'O' rings for fuel connector.
- New spark-plugs.
- Spark-plug spanner (or diesel injector spanner).
- Ratchet with extender and shifting spanner.
- Spare fuses, bung and shackle.
- Sharp knife, pliers and screwdrivers.
- Spare propeller nut, washer, split pins and socket for propeller nut.
- Steel wool to clean battery terminals.
- De-watering spray (RP7 or similar).

Safety and Weather Briefing

- Spare oil and funnel.
- Spare key and stop harness (kill switch lanyard).

Speed and Distance

The operation of a vessel can often be affected by physical conditions such as the direction of the wind, the depth of the water and visibility. When operating any type of vessel, always allow plenty of time and space in which to carry out any manoeuvre.

The operator is responsible at all times for keeping a proper lookout by using; sight, hearing and any appropriate means available. The operator must be fully aware of the boating environment, especially in bad weather, restricted visibility or darkness.

Safe Loading and Stability

Overloading is dangerous and may seriously reduce the stability and seaworthiness of your vessel. For example, overloading your boat may reduce freeboard making your boat less able to resist waves and more likely to be swamped.

Stability is different depending on what type of vessel you are operating.

Unless specified by the manufacturer (see owner's manual or builders/compliance plate) the maximum number of people that can be carried in a recreational vessel is represented in the table below:

Length of vessel	Maximum passengers*
Less than 3 m	Two people
3 m to less than 3.5 m	Three people
3.5 m to less than 4.5 m	Four people
4.5 m to less than 5 m	Five people
5 m to less than 5.5 m	Six people

Safety and Weather Briefing

5.5 m to less than 6 m	Seven people

In calculating the number of people on board a vessel:
- A child up to and including one year of age is not counted.
- Each child over one year and under 12 years is counted as 0.5 a person.

On recreational vessels with individual cockpits (for example, decked canoes or kayaks), the number of persons carried on the vessel must not exceed the number of individual cockpits, irrespective of the age of the person.

Warning

This is the maximum carrying capacity for good conditions. A reduction in the maximum number of persons should be made if planning to operate in adverse conditions or on the open sea.
- Weight of a person is assumed to be 75 kg per person, with an additional allowance of 15 kg per person for personal gear.
- A reduction in the number of persons should be made when equipment and supplies exceed total weight allocated.
- For vessels 6 m in length and more, refer to the manufacturer's recommendation for carrying capacity or contact your state safety authority.

Fit for purpose

The Marine Safety Regulations define fit for purpose as:
(a) the hull of the vessel is able to maintain watertight integrity
(b) there is no fuel leaking from the vessel's fuel system or engine
(c) the vessel's steering system controls the movement of the vessel
(d) the ventilation system used for ventilating a space or spaces in the vessel is functioning

(e) the material insulating machinery in the vessel from fire or flammable materials is fitted or undamaged
(f) the materials or items comprising part of the vessel's reserve buoyancy are fitted or undamaged
(g) the engine kill switches are fitted to the vessel and are operable.

12

Top 10 Reasons to Buy a Boat

With so many opportunities for boating fun available today, there's no reason why anyone cannot take advantage of the benefits that recreational boating has to offer.

How many of the reasons listed below are SIMILAR to your current line of thinking? I'm guessing most are!

1. **Boating Improves Quality of Life.**

It's a proven fact that recreational boating goes a long way towards improving your quality of life. The minute you start to move forward on a boat, you'll notice how easy it is to leave your troubles behind. Recreational boating is a constructive form of entertainment that reduces stress and provides enriching opportunities for self-discovery, whether it's learning how to water ski, fishing or simply enjoying the warm glow of an evening sunset with your partner.

2. **Boating is an Affordable Recreation Alternative.**

Are you under the impression that recreational boating is too expensive for your current budget? Think again. Some boats can be financed to meet most levels of affordability. Dedicated boat lenders will work with you to help you save money and get you the best financing package available.

3. **Water Access is Closer than You Think.**

Did you know that more than eight in ten Australians (85%) live within 50 kilometres of the coastline of Australia, a figure growing in recent decades? Most people living near the coast live in capital cities, seven of which are situated on the coast. This means that water access is a lot closer and more convenient than you might think.

4. **Boating Fun Helps You Bond with Friends and Family.**

In a study by the National Marine Manufacturers Association in the USA, fishing, cruising and relaxing with family and friends were listed by respondents as their top three favourite boating activities. In other words, to many people the best part about boating doesn't revolve around the latest water skiing tricks or the number of fish caught — the best part of boating is simply the opportunities it provides for boating fun with friends and family.

Recreational boating is quality time spent away from the television set and video games, creating an atmosphere that brings people together and creates fond memories to last a lifetime.

5. **Boating Helps Reduce Stress.**

We can't stress the statistics enough — numerous studies have shown that a little bit of boating fun each day can go a long way towards reducing stress. In fact, the National Marine Manufacturers Association survey in the USA reports that thousands of American households listed boating and fishing as both in the top-three of all stress-relieving activities.

6. Boating is Convenient.

As we pointed out above, since over 80% of Australians live a short drive from an accessible body of water, you can be enjoying the fresh air and water in no time. In fact, the convenience of boating makes it possible to hop on your boat for a mini-vacation whenever you feel like it, as an alternative to other family recreational activities which can quickly add up to become expensive and time-consuming.

7. Boating is an Engaging and Rewarding Activity.

Recreational boating offers lots of opportunities for personal growth. Whether you're instilling your child with extra confidence as they learn how to properly secure a line, or you're enjoying the delicate taste of fresh fish that you caught yourself, boating recreation provides many different rewards for all ages.

8. Boating is Good Exercise.

From a rigorous sailing excursion to an invigorating run on water skis, boating provides sporting enthusiasts with many active endeavours to choose from. In fact, simply breathing in the brisk wind coming off the water in itself can go a long ways towards strengthening one's constitution, not to mention the additional physical and psychological benefits in terms of relaxation and stress relief.

9. Recreational Boating is Easy to Learn:

If you're new to boating, take heart. With so many available boating classes and courses to choose from, you'll be out on the water before you know it. Whether you've always wanted to learn how to sail, or you're just interested in new ways to spend quality time with your family, a wealth of available boater education courses can make boating easier to learn than ever.

10. Boating is FUN:

Last, but definitely not least, one of the top reasons for boating is simply because it's so much fun. There are so many activities to explore when it comes to boating, whether you like to fish, water ski, snorkel, or simply enjoy relaxing on the water. Be sure to check out our boating activities page to learn more about all the different ways you too can experience boating fun.

FAMILY BOATING EXPERIENCE
This photo is used with permission from: St Kilda Boat Sales

Appendix A:
Glossary Of Terms

What does all this boating stuff mean?

Here is a terrific A-Z glossary of boating terms lovingly put together by the folk at Discover Boating USA (www.discoverboating.com) and myself throughout the course of writing this book.

This way when someone lays the lingo on you, you can understand what the heck they're talking about!

Q: Is there any RED PORT LEFT?

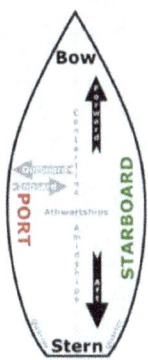

Glossary of boat speak

A

aerate
To force air and oxygen into live wells to keep fish or bait alive. Also, to force air under the running surface of a hull.

aft
The rear of the boat.

aft cabin
Sleeping quarters beneath the aft or rear section of the boat (sometimes called a mid-cabin when located beneath the helm).

alee
The side of a boat or object away from the direction of the wind.

aloft
Above deck in the rigging.

aluminium fish boat
Small, lightweight, durable trailerable boat constructed of aluminium that is either welded or riveted; generally used for freshwater fishing. Also known in Australia as a tinny.

amidships
Centre section of a boat.

anchorage
A location intended or suited for anchoring.

anodes

Small pieces of zinc or lead that attach to metal boat and engine components to help protect them from corrosion due to electrolysis, an effect caused when dissimilar metals are placed in a saltwater solution.

anti-fouling paint

A special paint applied to a boat's hull to prevent marine growth.

apparent wind

The direction and velocity of wind as felt in a moving boat.

astern

The direction toward or beyond the stern.

athwart

Perpendicular to a boat's centreline.

aweigh

An anchor that is off the bottom.

axle ratio

The relationship of revolutions of a tow vehicle's axle to that of its driveshaft or transaxle, e.g. 2.74:1.

B

backing down

Manoeuvring in reverse when offshore fishing while attempting to land a fish.

backstay

A support for the mast to keep it from falling forward.

Glossary Of Terms

bail

To remove water with a bucket or pump. Also, a component that controls fishing line on a spinning reel.

bait station

Area on a fishing boat for preparing bait.

baitwell

Compartment on a fishing boat for holding live bait, usually with a pump to circulate the water and an aerator to provide oxygen.

ballast

Weight added to the bottom of a boat to improve stability.

barra (bass) boat

Low-profile, outboard-powered boat, generally no more than 22 feet long and typically equipped with rod lockers, casting decks with pedestal seats and live wells. Also known as a Bass boat in the USA.

bay boat

Low-profile, inshore fishing boat intended for use in protected coastal waters, and frequently made with rolled-edge construction.

beach catamaran

Small, lightweight sailboat less than 25 feet long that can be easily launched and retrieved from a beach.

beam

Measurement of a boat at its widest point. Also, a transmitted radio, sonar or radar signal.

bear off

To turn away from the wind.

bearing
Direction to an object.

beating
Sailing upwind.

berth
A place to sleep aboard a boat. Also, a boat slip.

bilge
Lowest section inside a boat's hull where water collects.

bimini top
A canvas cover over the helm or cockpit area.

bitt
Vertical post extending above the deck to secure docking lines.

bluewater fishing boat
Mid-size to large deep-V boats suitable for offshore fishing. They are typically fitted with outriggers, fish boxes, aluminium towers, a host of electronics and large fuel tanks.

boat
Also known as vessel.

boom
A spar attached to a sail at its foot.

bow
Forward portion of a boat.

bow eye
A stainless steel U-bolt on a boat's bow stem used to secure tow lines or trailer winch hooks.

bow stop
Rubber blocks on a boat trailer into which the boat's stern rests.

bow-rider
A runabout boat with open-bow seating.

bowsprit
A spar extending forward of the bow on a sailboat.

breakaway lanyard
Emergency safety cable on a boat trailer that activates trailer brakes in the event the trailer comes detached from the tow vehicle while underway.

bridge clearance
Distance from waterline to a boat's highest point.

bulkhead
Transverse wall in a boat that usually bears weight and supplies hull support.

bunks
Long carpeted sections of a boat trailer that support the boat's weight.

buoy
An anchored floating object that serves as a navigation aid. Also used to mark a mooring spot.

burgee
Small flag that bears a yacht club's symbol.

C

camber
Curvature of a sail.

can buoy
Cylindrical navigation buoy with a flat top, generally green in colour.

capsize
To flip a boat over.

capstan
A winch used for hauling heavy objects such as anchors.

cast off
To unfasten all lines in preparation for departure.

casting platform
Elevated deck clear of obstruction used by anglers to make casts, often equipped with pedestal chairs.

catamaran
A twin hulled boat, either power or sail.

catboat
Small, simple sailboat with one mast and sail set far forward.

cavitation
Inefficient low-pressure pockets on propellers form bubbles that collapse against the blades resulting in premature wear.

centre console boat
Fishing boat with the helm station located amidships for maximum walk-through space around the perimeter of the boat.

Glossary Of Terms

centreboard

A keel-like pivoting device, typically in a trunk, that can be lowered or raised to act as a keel.

channel

The navigable portion of a waterway.

chart plotter

Electronic navigation device that displays charts for use in plotting a course.

chart recorder

An electronic depth sounder that records bottom structure data on paper.

charts

Paper or electronic navigation maps.

chine

Portion of the hull where the bottom and sides intersect (can be rounded or angled).

chopped fibreglass

Fibreglass strands cut and simultaneously mixed with resin by and applied to, a boat mould by using a chopper gun.

chumming

Placing fish or fish parts in the water to attract game fish.

class I hitch

Trailer hitch with a weight-carrying capacity up to 2,000 pounds; available as a bumper mount, step bumper or bumper/frame mount.

class II hitch

Frame-mounted trailer hitch with a weight-carrying capacity of up to 3,500 pounds.

class III hitch
Frame-mounted trailer hitch with a weight-carrying capacity of up to 5,000 pounds.

class IV hitch
Frame-mounted trailer hitch with a weight-carrying capacity of up to 10,000 pounds.

clears
PVC like clear curtains used in boat covers. However much better quality and purposely designed for marine use. UV treated. Protection from wind, rain and elements.

cleat
Hardware piece on a boat or a dock to which lines are attached.

clew
The after-most corner of a sail.

close-hauled
Sailing as close to the wind as possible.

coaming
A raised edge, as around the cockpit or around a hatchway, to keep water out.

coast guard safety pack
Basic safety gear required by federal law consisting of personal flotation devices, throwable flotation devices, visible distress signals, fire extinguisher and a horn, whistle or bell.

cockpit
Deck space for the crew of a boat, typically recessed.

Glossary Of Terms

colregs

Coast Guard term for the navigation rules of the road; full name is International Regulations for Preventing Collisions at Sea.

come about

To tack or change heading relative to the wind.

companionway

Entryway from the deck to the below deck cabin area.

convertible

A Bluewater fishing boat typically more than 35 feet long with a full cruising saloon, a fish-fighting cockpit and many other saltwater fishing features.

coring material

Any of a variety of lightweight materials used between layers of fibreglass laminates to add strength.

corinthian

Amateur yachtsman.

counter rotation

The act of two propellers spinning in opposite directions on a single shaft.

coupler

Component on a boat trailer that connects to the hitch ball.

course

Direction in which a boat is steered.

cruiser

A boat with overnight accommodations.

cuddy cabin
Below deck accommodation in the bow area for overnighting and stowage.

cure
Hardening process for resin-soaked fibreglass laminates.

curtains
Attachable front and side enclosures that protect the helm area from weather.

cutter
Single-masted sailboat similar to a sloop, but with the mast farther aft to allow for a double headsail.

D

daggerboard
A keel-like device that is manually raised and lowered vertically without using a hinge.

davit
A small crane used to hoist a boat or dinghy or other object.

day sailing
To go sailing for a few hours on a small, open sailboat.

daysailer
Small, open sailboat sometimes raced or short-distanced cruised, primarily used for recreational sailing.

dead ahead
Directly ahead of the bow.

deadrise
Degrees of V-shape hull angle measured at the transom of planing powerboats.

deck boat
Blunt-bowed power boat generally characterized by an open deck and generous passenger seating.

deep-V
A hull shape characterized by a sharp deadrise, typically more than 20 degrees.

depth sounder
Electronic sonar device that displays water depth.

deviation
The amount of error from displaying magnetic north in a boat's compass caused by the boat's own magnetic interference.

differential GPS (DGPS)
A highly accurate global positioning system (GPS) that utilizes a differential radio beacon and receiver to compute and correct the error of all visible satellites sending data to a conventional GPS unit.

dinette
A small dining area usually consisting of a table and facing bench seats; it can often be converted into a berth.

dinghy
A small sailboat often raced that can be sailed on and off a beach. Also a tender, either rowed or equipped with power, used to go to and from a larger vessel.

direct drive
An engine configuration in which the drive shaft runs in a straight driveline through the bottom of the hull.

displacement
The weight of water displaced by a hull. Also, a type of hull that smoothly displaces water as opposed to riding on top of it.

displacement hull
A hull shape designed to run through water rather than on top of it in the manner of a planing hull.

downrigger
A gunwale-mounted weighted line device used for deep-water trolling.

draft
Vertical distance a boat penetrates the water.

drogue
A parachute-like sea anchor.

dry weight
Weight of the boat without fuel and fresh water.

dual-console boat
A type of boat with twin dashboards separated by a centreline walk-through deck leading to the bow.

E

EPIRB

Acronym for emergency positioning indicating radio beacon. When this electronic device is activated it transmits a radio signal with user registration data and positioning information to a network of satellites that assist the Coast Guard in conducting an emergency rescue.

express cruiser

A cruising boat without a deck-level salon. Sometimes called a Sunbridge cruiser.

F

fathom

Nautical depth measurement equalling six feet.

fender

A cylindrical or round cushion used to protect the hull sides of a boat, typically used when tied up at dock.

fetch

To clear a buoy, point of land or object without having to make a tack.

fibreglass

Glass fibres either loose or woven, reinforced with resin and used in the construction of many boats.

fighting chair

A fix-mounted chair used to help land large game fish on Bluewater fishing boats equipped with a footrest, gimbal-mounted rod holder, safety harness and other fish-fighting gear.

fin keel
A keel shaped like the fin of a fish that is shorter and deeper than a full-length keel.

fishfinder
Electronic device that uses sonar (echo sounder) to locate and display fish on a monitor.

fix
The position of a boat recorded in coordinates or bearings.

flare
A pyrotechnic device used to indicate distress. Also, the outward curvature of the sides on the bow of a boat.

flat-bottom boat
Type of boat or hull shape with very little or no deadrise.

flats boat
Type of small, inshore saltwater fishing boat with moderate deadrise and draft, usually equipped with a raised platform aft used by a guide pushing a long pole to silently manoeuvre the boat through shallow tidal water.

flybridge
Raised, second-story helm station, often located above the primary helm.

following sea
Wave pattern running in the same direction as the boat.

foot
The bottom edge of a sail.

fore
Located at the front of a boat.

foredeck

Forward part of the main deck, ahead of the superstructure.

foul-weather gear

Jacket, pants and hat used during inclement weather.

founder

To sink.

four-cycle engine

A petrol or diesel-powered internal combustion engine that takes four-cycles or strokes of the piston to complete its power phase. Also called four-stroke engine.

frame-mount hitch

Hitch fastened to the frame of a tow vehicle.

freeboard

Vertical distance between the waterline and the top of the hull side.

furling

Rolling or folding a sail on its boom.

G

gaff

A metal pole with a hooked end used to boat a fish. Also a pole or spar that holds the upper portion of a four-sided sail.

galley

The kitchen area on a boat.

gelcoat
A combination of resin and pigment that comprises the smooth outside coating of a fibreglass boat.

genoa
An overlapping jib.

genset
Another name for a petrol or diesel powered electric generator.

give way
Yield to other traffic.

GPS
Acronym for global positioning system, a satellite-based navigation system that uses transmitted signals and mathematical triangulation to pinpoint location.

gross axle weight rating (GAWR)
The maximum weight an axle is designed to carry.

gross combined weight rating (GCWR)
The maximum allowable weight of a fully loaded tow vehicle plus its fully loaded trailer, including passengers and cargo.

gross trailer weight (GTW)
The maximum allowable weight of trailer and its cargo.

gross vehicle mass (GVM)
The maximum allowable weight of a fully equipped tow vehicle including passengers and cargo.

gunkhole
To explore creeks, coves, marshes or other shallow areas near shore.

Glossary Of Terms

gunwale
The upper edge of the side of a boat.

gybe
Also spelled jibe. To change the course of a boat so that the boom swings over to the opposite side.

H

halyard
Line used to hoist a spar or sail.

harbor master
The person at a harbour in charge of anchorages, berths and harbour traffic.

hard chine
A sharp-angle at the intersection of the hull's side and bottom.

hard over
Turning the steering wheel or tiller all the way in one direction.

hard-top
A large fibreglass roof or platform over the helm area.

hatch
A deck opening.

hauling
To lift a boat from the water.

Glossary Of Terms

hawse pipe

Fittings in the deck or gunwale through which the anchor rode or dock lines run.

head

Toilet facilities or room where they are located.

head seas

Waves coming from the direction a boat is heading.

heading

The direction a boat is pointed.

headsail

Any sail set forward of the mast.

headway

Forward motion of a boat in the water.

heave

To pull on a line. Also to throw a line.

heaving to

Setting the sails so the boat makes little headway, either used in a storm or a waiting situation.

heel

To temporarily tip or lean to one side.

helm

Area of a boat where operational controls are located.

high-performance boat

A type of boat capable of running at high speeds, often equipped with high-horsepower and exotic propulsion systems, sometimes used for racing.

hike
To lean out on the windward side of a sailboat to achieve optimal speed by offsetting heeling.

hitch
Steel framework on a tow vehicle used to hook up a trailer.

hitch ball
The ball-shaped component of the hitch that fits into the trailer coupler.

holding tank
Storage tank for grey water.

houseboat
A large, flat-bottom boat with square sides and house-like characteristics, such as comfortable furniture and living accommodations.

hull
The structural body of the boat that rests in the water.

I

inboard engine
An internal combustion engine often mounted amidships that runs a drive shaft through the hull bottom.

inboard/outboard (I/O)
See sterndrive.

inflatable
Capable of being inflated either with air, as in a life raft or life vest.

inflatable boat
A type of boat with air chambers into which air is pumped either manually or automatically for buoyancy, some having rigid bottoms.

inner liner
Smooth-finished, moulded fibreglass structure adjacent to the inside portion of the hull.

inverter
Device that changes 12-, 24- or 32-volt direct current (DC) from a battery to 120-volt alternating current (AC).

J

jack plate
A mounting device for an outboard motor that enables operators to vertically raise or lower the motor, thereby controlling propeller depth in the water.

jet boat
A boat powered by an engine with a water-pump used to create propulsion.

jib
Triangular sail projecting ahead of the mast.

jibe
See gybe.

K

keel

The bottom-most portion or longitudinal centreline of a hull.

ketch

A sailboat similar in appearance to a yawl with a tall main mast and a shorter mizzen mast ahead of the rudder post.

kicker motor

A small auxiliary outboard motor.

kill switch

A switch with a lanyard that automatically shuts off an engine if disconnected.

kite fishing

A technique that involves attaching a fishing line to a kite to present bait at a distance from the boat.

knot

Speed measured in nautical miles per hour. Converted as: 1 knot per hour = 1.852kilometres per hour or 1.51 miles per hour

L

laminate

A single layer of material used in multi-layered fibreglass construction.

lamination schedule

A list of the sequential layers of materials used in fibreglass construction.

latitude
Geographic distance north or south of the equator expressed in degrees and minutes.

leaning post
Wide, padded bolster at the helm used instead of or in lieu of conventional seats.

lee
Direction toward which the wind blows.

lee side
The side of an object that is sheltered from the wind.

leeway
To slip sideways downwind while moving forward.

lifeline
Safety lines on deck that are grabbed to prevent falling overboard.

list
A continuous lean to one side due to improper weight distribution.

livewell
Compartment on a fishing boat designed to keep fish or bait alive.

LOA
Length overall; the distance between the most forward part of the boat and the most aft part.

locker
A stowage compartment, whether equipped with a lock or not.

longitude
Geographic distance east or west of the prime meridian expressed in degrees and minutes.

Loran C
Electronic navigation system that measures the time difference in the reception of radio signals from land-based transmitters.

luff
The leading edge of a sail.

M

mainsail
The largest regular sail on a sailboat.

make fast
To secure a line.

marinisation
The addition of marine components to automotive engines.

mast
Vertical spar that supports sails.

MAYDAY
A radio distress call.

megayacht
A large, luxurious yacht, typically longer than 100 feet

midships
Location near the centre of a boat.

mizzen mast
A shorter mast located aft of the main mast on a yawl or ketch.

modified-V hull
A modification of the deep-V hull shape with a deadrise of less than 20 degrees.

mold
A hollow reinforced cavity that is the mirror-image or reverse-image of the boat and into which fibreglass, gel coat and resin are laid during composite-hull construction.

monohull
A boat with a single hull.

mooring
Permanent ground tackle fixed to a buoy that boats can tie to.

motorsailer
A hybrid boat that has sails and powerful engines.

motoryacht
A large powerboat greater than 40 feet with luxurious interior accommodations for long-range cruising.

multihull
A boat with more than one hull, such as a catamaran or trimaran.

N

nautical mile
A distance of 6,076.12 feet, 1,852 meters, 1.852 kilometres or 1.151

miles. Which is about 15 percent longer than a statute mile. Equivalent to one minute of latitude on a navigation chart.

nun buoy

Conical navigation buoy that is usually red.

O

outboard bracket

Support device for mounting outboard engines that extends aft of the transom. Often also known as auxiliary bracket for the mounting of the auxiliary engine.

outboard motor

Internal combustion engine mounted at the transom that incorporates motor, driveshaft and propeller.

outdrive

The lower unit of a stern-drive motor that houses the drive gears and to which the propeller fastens.

outrigger

Poles designed to spread out fishing lines and keep them from tangling while trolling. Also known as game pole.

overboard

Over the side of a boat and into the water.

P

personal flotation device (PFD)
A safety vest or jacket capable of keeping an individual afloat.

personal watercraft (PWC)
A small, lightweight craft designed to be either sat-on or stood-on with motorcycle-like handlebars and squeeze throttle, usually jet-propelled. Often called a Jet ski.

piling
A post driven into the ground below the waterline to support a pier, dock, etc.

pilot house
A fully enclosed helm compartment.

pitch
Theoretical distance a propeller would travel in one revolution. Also, the rise and fall of a boat's bow and stern.

planing hull
A boat hull designed to ride on top of the water rather than ploughing through it.

pleasure boating
Recreational day boating in runabouts, deck boats, pontoon boats, bow riders and sport boats.

plot
To plan a navigation course using a chart.

poling platform
Small elevated stand on a flat boat used by a fisherman to silently pole through shallow water and scout for fish.

pontoon boat
A type of boat with a flat deck attached to airtight flotation tubes or logs.

port
The left side of a boat when facing the bow. Also, a marina harbour or commercial dock.

power catamaran
A multi-hulled powerboat with two identical side-by-side hulls.

power cruiser
A powerboat with overnight accommodations, typically up to 40 feet long.

propeller
A rotating multi-blade device that propels a boat through the water.

pulpit
Forward deck and railing structure at the bow of a boat.

PWC
See personal watercraft.

Q

quarter
The after side of a boat from amidships to stern.

quartering
The practice of aiming the boat's bow at a 45-degree angle to oncoming waves.

quarters
Living and sleeping areas of a vessel.

R

racer
A sailboat designed primarily for speed and competition with a minimum of built-in creature comforts.

racer/cruiser
A fast sailboat designed with comfortable accommodations.

radar
Electronic device using high frequency radio waves to detect objects and display their positions on a monitor.

range
Distance a boat can travel at cruising speed on a tank of fuel. Also, the distance to an object. Lastly, in intra-coastal navigation, a set of two markers that, when lined up one behind the other, indicate the deepest part of the channel.

reach
To sail across the wind.

ready about
Last warning given by a helmsman before tacking and turning the bow into the wind, notifying the crew that the boom and sail will cross the boat.

receiver box
Part of a hitch that receives and holds the hitch bar or shank.

Glossary Of Terms

receiver hitch
A hitch with a receiver from which a hitch bar or shank can be removed.

resin
Liquid substance used in fibreglass composite construction that, when combined with a catalyst, bonds laminate materials together.

reverse chine
A chine that angles downward from the hull designed to direct spray out and away from the boat.

rib (rigid inflatable boat)
An inflatable boat fitted with a rigid bottom.

rigging
Wire cables, rods, lines, hardware and other equipment that support and control the mast and spars.

rocket launcher
A device designed for a fishing boat that bolts to the cockpit floor or is incorporated into a bench seat, to hold multiple fishing rods.

rod holder
Device designed to safely and securely hold fishing rods either vertically or horizontally.

rode
Line, chain, cable or any combination of these used to connect the anchor to the boat.

rolled-edge skiff
A fishing boat designed to run in coastal waters constructed of a simple, one-piece fibreglass hull without a top deck and characterized by rounded top edges without true gunwales.

roller trailer
A trailer outfitted with rollers instead of bunks.

rubrail
Protective outer bumper that runs around the boat at the point where the top deck meets the hull.

rudder
Underwater fin mounted below the hull near the stern that controls boat steering.

runabout
A kind of small, lightweight, freshwater pleasure craft intended for day use.

running lights
Required navigation lights that a vessel uses at night to indicate position and status.

running rigging
Lines used in the setting and trimming of sails.

S

sacrificial anodes
Small pieces of zinc or lead attached to a metal boat and engine components to help protect them from corrosion due to electrolysis, an effect caused when dissimilar metals are placed in a saltwater solution.

safety chains
Legally mandated chains that connect the trailer to the tow vehicle as a safety measure in case the coupler detaches.

safety harness
A harness worn by a boater attached to the boat with a tether to reduce the chances of going overboard.

sag
To slide or drift off course.

sail plan
Arrangement of sails on a boat.

sailboat
A boat that is at least partially propelled by capturing the force of wind in sails.

saloon
Full-sized, well-appointed cabin on the main deck level of a motor-yacht, convertible or mega-yacht used for entertaining.

saltwater fishing boat
Any fishing boat used in the ocean or coastal waters that's specially equipped to handle the harsh saltwater environment.

schooner
A large sailboat with two or more masts where the foremast is shorter than aft mainmast.

scope
The ratio of anchor rope to vertical depth.

scud
To run before the wind in bad weather.

scuppers
Gravity fed drain in a boat to allow water to drain out and overboard.

Glossary Of Terms

scuttle
To cut holes or open ports to purposely let water in to make a boat sink.

scuttlebutt
Gossip. So named after a water cask around which sailors used to gather and drink.

sea anchor
A canvas, cone-shaped device deployed to keep the bow headed into the wind to help safely ride out a storm. Also called a drogue.

sea cock
Through-hull fitting with a valve between the interior and the exterior of the boat.

seaworthy
Ability to handle rough weather. Also called sea-kindly.

sedan cruiser
A type of large boat equipped with a saloon and a raised helm or bridge.

self-bailing
Drains water overboard automatically.

semi-displacement hull
A hull shape with soft chines or a rounded bottom that enables the boat to achieve minimal planing characteristics.

sheer
Line of the deck or gunwale from bow to stern as viewed from outside the boat.

sheet
Line used to trim a sail.

Glossary Of Terms

shroud

Mast support rigging, usually a wire that runs from the mast to the side of the boat.

side console

A dash-panel unit affixed to the side of a boat. If only one, helm controls are affixed to it.

skeg

A fin or vertical projection below the hull that provides directional stability. Also, a fin-like projection at the bottom of an outboard.

skiff

A small, simple, shallow-draft boat.

skiing/wakeboarding boat

Low profile, pleasure boats with minimal deadrise specifically designed for waterskiing and/or wakeboarding. These boats are usually characterised by an inboard engine and a towing pylon. Wakeboard boats are often equipped with a tower or extremely tall pylon to fasten the tow line in a manner to aid vertical jumping and water-ballast devices to increase the weight of the boat.

slip

A boat berth between two piers or floats. Also, the slight loss of efficient power delivery as a propeller spins in the water.

sloop

A single-masted sailboat in which the mast is set forward of midships.

sole

The deck floor.

sonar

A method to locate objects and determine distance by transmitting sound waves through water and measuring the time it takes the echo to bounce back. Used in depth finders and fishfinders.

sounding

Charted water depth.

spar

Masts, booms, gaffs and poles used in sailboat rigging.

sportfish

A type of bluewater fishing boat with at least two sleeping cabins and many dedicated fish-fighting features.

spring line

A docking line attached amidships to control fore and aft movement.

stand by

An order to crewmen to be ready, be prepared.

stand on

Maintain course and speed.

standing rigging

The shrouds and stays that support the mast, but are not adjusted while working a boat.

starboard

The right side of the boat looking toward the bow.

stateroom

A room with sleeping quarters, a cabin.

statute mile

Distance of 5,280 feet, the standard measure of distance on land and most inland waterways.

stay
Wire, rod or other rigging that runs fore and aft of the mast.

stem
The most forward section of the hull.

step
Socket that holds the base of the mast.

stepped hull
A high-performance hull design with lateral notches, or steps, in the keel.

stern
Aft portion of a boat.

sterndrive
Propulsion system composed of an inboard engine connected to a steerable drive unit extending through a cut-out in the transom.

stow
To put an object away onboard a boat, to store.

strakes
Small linear protrusions that run longitudinally on both sides of the keel to give a planing hull lift and lateral stability.

stringers
Internal beams and braces that give a fibreglass hull structural support.

surge brakes
Hydraulic trailer brake system activated by the sudden inertia of a trailer pushing against the tow vehicle during a hard stop.

Glossary Of Terms

swamp

To fill a boat with water.

sway

Side-to-side wandering of a trailer under tow.

swim platform

A wide platform at the transom equipped with a ladder to help ease the effort of reboarding after going into the water.

T

T-top

Short, aluminium tower with overhead canvas to protect the helm.

tack

The lower corner of a sail. Also, each leg of a zigzag course.

tender

See dinghy.

through-hull

A fitting or object that goes all the way through a hull.

tiller

A bar connected to the rudder and used to steer the boat.

tiller handle outboard

A small, outboard motor that uses a handle fitted with engine controls to steer instead of a steering wheel.

tongue jack

Adjustable jack on the trailer tongue that raises and lowers the coupler.

Glossary Of Terms

tongue weight

The measurement of trailer weight when loaded with a boat on the hitch ball.

topsides

The hull above the waterline. Also, everything above deck as opposed to below deck.

tow rating

Maximum weight a vehicle is rated to tow. Refer to vehicle owner's manual.

trailer tongue

Forward portion of a trailer where the coupler is mounted.

trailer winch

Device that uses a crank and cable to assist in launching and retrieving a boat.

transducer

An electronic sensing device mounted in a boat's bilge or at the bottom of the transom to provide data for a depth sounder.

transom

The rear section of the hull connecting the two sides.

transom shower

A plastic hose and shower head located near the transom that draws from a fresh water supply.

trawler

A pleasure boat more than 25 feet in length with a displacement hull.

Glossary Of Terms

trim

The way a boat floats in relation to the horizon, bow up, bow down or even. Also, to adjust a boat's horizontal running angle by directing the outboard or stern drive's thrust up or down. Also, to set a sail in correct relation to the wind.

trim tabs

Hydraulically adjusted horizontal plates located on the bottom of the transom that control the trim angle of a boat at speed.

trimaran

A type of boat with three side-by-side hulls, the centre of which is usually larger with crew accommodations.

trolling

To fish by towing an array of baited lines or lures behind the boat.

true wind

Direction and velocity of wind as measured on land, distinct from apparent wind.

tuna tower

Tall aluminium tower used for spotting fish in the distance, often equipped with a second set of helm controls.

two-cycle engine (2 stroke)

A petrol or diesel-powered internal combustion engine that takes two cycles or strokes of the piston to complete its power phase. Also called two-stroke engine.

U

underway

A boat in motion.

utility boat

A type of small, open powerboat, constructed of either fibreglass or aluminium, with minimal features. These include jon boats, skiffs and work boats.

V

V-berth

A bed or berth located in the bow that has a V-shape.

V-drive

Propulsion system where the drive shaft initially runs forward into a gear box and then runs aft and down through the hull. The driveline forms a V-shape with the gear box at the pivot point.

vacuflush

Brand of toilet flushing system for boats.

variation

Compass variable that accounts for the difference in degrees between true north and magnetic north.

ventilation

Air introduced into a spinning propeller from the water's surface.

VHF

Very high frequency; a bandwidth designation commonly used by marine radios.

vybak

Brand name of the PVC like clear curtains used in boat covers. However, much better quality and purposely designed for marine use. UV treated.

W

wake

Waves created by a moving boat.

walkaround

A type of offshore fishing boat with a small to mid-size cabin and a perimeter deck that allows easy passage around the entire boat.

waterline

The intersection of the hull and the surface of the water.

waypoint

The coordinates of a specific location.

weigh

To raise anchor.

windlass

Rotating drum device used for hauling line or chain to raise and lower an anchor. Often called electric anchor.

working sails

Sails used in normal winds.

X

Y

yachting
To cruise in a motor yacht that typically ranges from 40- to 89- feet long.

yaw
To veer off course.

Z

zinc anodes
Small pieces of zinc or lead that attach to metal boat and engine components to help protect them from corrosion due to electrolysis, an effect caused when dissimilar metals are placed in a saltwater solution.

Appendix B:

Compliant Boats

An understanding of the Australian Builders Plate (ABP)

Look out for Australian Builders Plates on new Australian made and imported recreational boats, including owner built boats. The National Standard for the Australian Builders Plate for Recreational Boats is overseen by the Australian Recreational Boating Safety Committee (ARBSC). The ARBSC took over this responsibility from the National Marine Safety Committee (NMSC) in 2011. For further information about the ABP please contact your local marine jurisdiction.

The ABP aims to make boating safer by providing information about the capability of boats including: the maximum number of people and load they can safely carry; the maximum outboard engine power and the buoyancy performance for smaller boats.

The information below dated February 2012, is attributed to:
www.nmsc.gov.au

Frequently Asked Questions for the General Public

The ABP and the law

1. Is the ABP required by law?

All Australian states apply the National Standard for the ABP for Recreational Boats (the ABP standard) either through Maritime Safety or the consumer protection law. There are some differences between states in the mechanism for enforcing compliance as a result of the way the local legislation is drafted; however, if somebody is trying to sell you a new boat without an ABP they may be in breach of the law and you may not be able to register it.

2. When was the law introduced?

The law was introduced at different times in each state. A summary of those dates is given on the NMSC website on the main ABP page. You should check the details with your local Marine Safety Agency.

Implementation of the ABP plate

3. Which boats are required to have an ABP?

New boats are required to have an ABP plate with the exception of: an amphibious vehicle; a canoe, kayak, surf ski or similar vessel designed to be powered by paddle; a rowing shell used for racing or rowing training; a sailboard or sail kite; a surf row boat; a hydrofoil or hovercraft; a race boat; a sailing vessel; a submersible; or an aquatic toy.

A sailing boat with an auxiliary engine is exempt from the requirement to have an ABP fitted.

Vessels subject to a Certificate of Survey, Personal Water Craft (PWC) and

Compliant Boats

Inflatable boats must comply with different requirements.

What about second hand boats without an ABP? Most states do not require a second hand vessel to have an ABP. Please check with your local marine safety authority.

4. What labelling does a Personal Water Craft (PWC) require?

The ABP is not required on a PWC designed to carry up to two people.

An ABP is required on PWCs intended to carry three or more persons unless the craft already has information clearly and permanently marked that states:
1. The maximum number of persons the vessel may carry, as recommended by the builder.
2. The total mass of persons and equipment (expressed in kilograms) that the craft is designed to carry, as recommended by the builder

5. Who can determine the information on an ABP?

The information on an ABP must be determined by a competent person.

A competent person is defined as a person who has acquired through training, qualification, experience, or a combination of these, the knowledge and skills enabling that person to competently determine the information on a Builders Plate.

The competent person is either:
1. The builder;
2. The importer; or
3. A third-party competent person.

In general, a commercial boat builder is deemed to be a competent person for the purpose of the ABP standard. In the case of an owner-builder or importer, they may not meet the definition of a competent person, in which case a third-party competent person may need to be engaged to determine the information. Where this occurs, the name of the third-party competent person should be shown on the ABP, along with that of the builder or importer. In some states, the Marine Safety Agency maintains a list of approved third-parties who can act as a competent person for the purpose of complying with the ABP standard. Any person whose name appears on the plate is assuming responsibility for the information on that plate.

Examples
- Built by Sunhope Boats, Australia.
- Imported by RayStan Holdings, Australia.
- Information approved by E.R. Smith, Naval Architect, Sydney, Aust.

6. What happens if a dealer modifies a boat prior to sale?

If a dealer modifies the boat so the information on the plate is no longer correct, then the dealer will need to ensure a new plate is placed on the boat prior to sale.

The dealer can request this to be done by the builder, if the builder is agreeable, or alternatively by a competent person.

Boats built overseas

7. What about boats built overseas?

Regardless of where the boat was built, it will still be required to comply with the ABP standard. If you privately import a boat into Australia you will be treated as the builder of the boat for the purpose of the ABP legislation and will need to fit it with an ABP.

8. Is a US or European Compliance Plate acceptable as an alternative to an ABP for a typical boat?

No.

Except for the special treatment of inflatable boats and PWCs mentioned above, overseas compliance plates are not an acceptable alternative to an ABP. For one thing, if the information on the plate proves to be false a company located overseas is beyond the reach of the applicable Australian laws.

Hull Identification Numbers (HINs) and the ABP

9. If a boat has a HIN, does it also need an ABP?

Yes.

The HIN and the ABP serve different purposes and provide different information. The requirement to put an ABP on a boat is in addition to any existing requirements relating to HINs. See below for HIN explanation.

Location of the ABP

10. Where do I find the ABP on a boat?

The ABP standard states the ABP is required to be placed in a position where it will be readily visible to the operator of the boat when getting the boat underway, preferably in the cockpit or near the steering position. Placing the ABP on the outside of the transom of a boat is not acceptable.

11. What about boats with more than one steering position?

The plate is only required in the primary steering position, however there is nothing preventing multiple plates or a warning plate at an access point such as on a ladder to the flybridge.

Plate Construction and Design

12. How is the plate fixed to the boat?

The standard states that the plate has to be permanently fixed to the boat so it is resistant to removal without leaving an obvious mark.

Examples of ways in which a plate might be attached include riveting, gluing, embedding, engraving or printing the plate directly onto the boat, provided that whatever method is used the plate is permanently fixed to the boat.

13. Does the plate have to be a particular shape or size?

No.

The ABP standard does not specify that the plate has to be a particular size or shape. The standard does, however, specify the size of the text and symbols to be used on the plate. The standard also specifies the information on the plate.

The plate can be any size and shape provided the plate complies with the requirements relating to text, symbol size and legibility, and displays all the information required by the standard. The standard provides a sample plate that meets the requirements to assist manufacturers in designing their own plate.

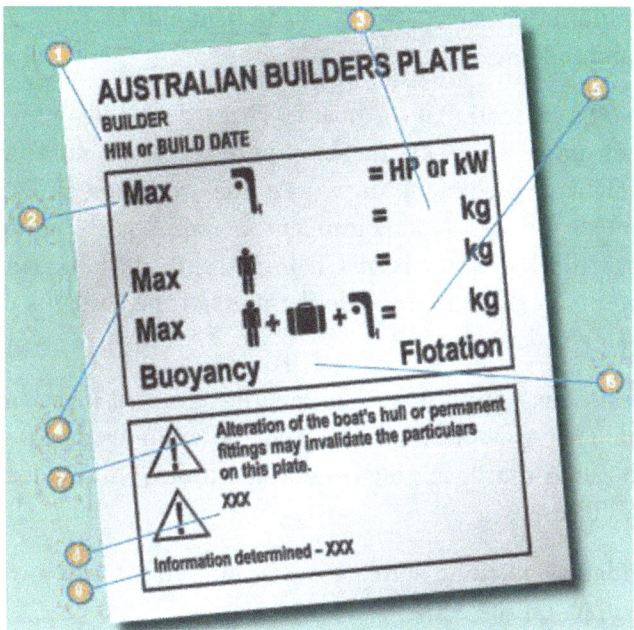

This is a sample of an ABP for a boat less than six meters with an outboard motor.

For further details, please refer to the National Standard for Australian Builders Plate for Recreational Boats. The list below describes in detail what is on an ABP.

1) **Name of the person approving information on the plate, normally the builder or importer, and the capacity in which they approved the information and either the Hull Identification Number (HIN) or the year built.**

2) **Maximum outboard engine power rating for which the boat has been designed and tested, expressed in kilowatts or horsepower.**

3) **Maximum outboard engine weight for which the boat has been designed and tested (expressed in kilograms), including the weight of any auxiliary outboard.**

Honey, let's buy a BOAT! 311

Compliant Boats

4) Maximum number of persons on the boat expressed as a whole number and in kilograms.

5) The maximum load that the boat has been designed and tested to carry when underway. This includes persons, maximum outboard engine weight allowed including any auxiliary engines, and carry-on equipment such as personal equipment, personal safety equipment, spare parts, tools, dry provisions, fishing tackle, portable tanks and their contents. It does not include the mass of the contents of fixed fuel or water tanks.

6) For boats less than 6 metres in length there will be a buoyancy statement. The terms used may be basic flotation or level flotation. After July 2006 the term "inadequate flotation" will no longer be permitted for use.

7) A mandatory warning statement that alterations may invalidate the particulars on the ABP.

8) The person approving information on the plate may also add an optional person/load capacity warning statement or other safety information. Examples can include: "Warning — the recommended maximum persons to be carried on the Flybridge should not exceed 2 persons or 150 kilograms" or "Warning — the recommended maximum load should be reduced in bad weather or when the boat is operated offshore. Refer to the owner's manual before operation."

9) The standard used to determine the information provided on the plate. For example, "information determined — AS 1799".

14. Is the same style of plate used for boats less than six metres, and those six metres or more in length?

The standard requires different plates for vessels six metres or more in length from those less than six metres in length.

Compliant Boats

Boats less than six metres in length require buoyancy information; whereas boats that are six metres or more in length are not required to state their buoyancy.

In principle the more onerous plate (ie: the one for vessels under six metres) could be used on all vessels; however in practice it may be simpler to use different plates.

Motors

15. If I buy a boat without an engine, will the ABP still have the section relating to the power rating completed?

The ABP standard requires that all sections be completed correctly. For boats that do not have inboard engines this includes the maximum outboard motor power and mass that the hull can safely handle. This allows the owner of the vessel to fit an appropriate sized motor at a later date.

16. Does the power rating have to be in kilowatts?

No.

The ABP standard states that the maximum power capacity can be expressed in either horsepower (hp) (HP) or kilowatts (kW). The mass of the outboard motor must however, be specified in kilograms.

17. What happens if I fit an auxiliary outboard to the boat?

The information about the maximum outboard motor power rating applies only to the boat's primary motor. The power of any reserve outboard is excluded.

However, the mass of the auxiliary motor would need to be counted when the owner assesses whether or not the proposed loading is within the maximum load capacity of the boat.

Maximum load and passenger capacity

18. What is included in the maximum load capacity?

The maximum load capacity represents the maximum mass a boat has been designed and tested to safely carry when underway, determined in accordance with selected technical standards. This includes the mass of persons, the outboard, including any auxiliary outboard, portable fuel tanks, and carry on equipment such as personal equipment, personal safety equipment, spare parts, tools, dry provisions, fishing tackle, portable tanks and their contents, etc. It does not include the mass of the contents of fixed fuel and water tanks when full.

19. What does the maximum passenger capacity mean?

The maximum passenger capacity is the recommended number of passengers the boat can safely carry, including their personal gear, based on mass. This number is necessarily an estimate because human beings don't all weigh the same. The permissible technical standards used to calculate the maximum load capacity (the Australian Standard, the US standard and the ISO standards used in Europe) all give more or less the same results for a given boat. However, the standards each use different masses for a typical person. Most standards express the result as the number of adults the boat can safely carry. The Australian Standard bases this on 80kg per person, however the US standard assumes a mix of adults and children and comes up with an average mass of around 65kg.

Symbols

20. Which symbols are used on the ABP?

Any symbol used shall be as specified in ISO 11192, or as illustrated in the ABP Standard.

Compliant Boats

Symbols that may be used include: an outboard engine symbol, a person symbol, a suitcase symbol, and a warning symbol.

If symbols are used:

- The outboard engine symbol shall be used to display information about a boat's maximum outboard power capacity and mass.
- The person symbol shall be used to display information about a boat's maximum passenger capacity as the number of adults and their total mass.
- The person symbol combined with the suitcase symbol and the outboard symbol (in the case of a boat not fitted with an inboard engine) shall be used to display the boat's maximum load capacity.
- The warning symbol shall be used to display warning information.

Warning Statements

21. What constitutes a warning statement on the ABP?

A warning statement cautions the user. The ABP specifies one mandatory warning that must be displayed on all boats, with the following words being used:

"Alteration of the boat's hull or permanent fittings may invalidate the particulars on this plate." Builders may include additional warnings that are relevant to the boat in question. For boats with a Flybridge, the warning statement may provide maximum passenger numbers to be carried on the Flybridge or a warning statement may refer the user to the owner's manual before operating the boat.

Example of warning statement that refers to Flybridge boats: "WARNING — The recommended maximum number of persons to be carried on the Flybridge at any time should not exceed 2 persons or 160 Kilograms."

If a warning is used, it must be consistent with any limitations expressed or implied with the standards used.

Standard to Be Shown on Plate

22. Does the plate have to show the standard used to determine the information provided on the plate?

Yes.

The name of the standard used to determine the information on the plate has to be shown on the plate.

This should be expressed as: "Information determined (insert name of appropriate standard)." The name of the standard may be expressed as the standard number or abbreviation by which the standard is commonly known, rather than its title (ie: AS 1799, ISO 12217, ABYC).

EXAMPLE:

"Information determined - AS 1799."

Flotation

23. What is meant by basic and level flotation?

Basic Flotation

The ABP Standard defines basic flotation as "a flotation system that will keep a boat carrying its maximum load from sinking when swamped, assuming the occupants of the boat have left it and are in the water clinging to it. With basic flotation the swamped boat may float at any attitude". This is a general definition to explain the concept.

Level Flotation

Level flotation is defined in the ABP standard as being "a flotation system that will keep a boat carrying its maximum load from sinking when swamped, assuming the occupants remain within the boat and supported by the flotation system. The flotation system must be such that it will keep the swamped boat floating level and prevent it from capsizing in calm water. Level flotation does not provide a self-righting capacity, but in calm water should allow bailing of the boat."

FOR MORE INFORMATION
Contact your local Maritime Safety Agency. Imp

Hull Identification Number (HIN) Explained

US – XJL 18098 D 6 06

| Country Code | MIC Code Manufacturers identity Code | Build Serial Number | Prod. Month | Prod. Year | Model Year |

Compliant Boats

Country Code:

AU - Australia

IT - Italy

FR- France

US - USA

NZ - New Zealand

Production Month:

A – January

B – February

C – March

D – April

E – May

F – June

G – July

H – August

I – September

J – October

K – November

L - December

Appendix C:

Captain's Briefing - Things to know

Must read information for the owner, skipper and crew.

Boat Licensing

Boat licence requirements vary in each state and territory of Australia

Each state and territory within Australia has different laws regarding commercial and recreational boat licences. A motor boat operator can select their state or territory and find detailed information on the boat licence requirements in order to get out on the water and boating safely around the Australian coast.

Some other frequently asked questions are:

Captain's Briefing - Things to know

Can I use a boat licence in another state or territory?

Most states and territories recognise the boating licences of other states and territories for a period of time (usually around three months), but be sure to check with the Maritime/Boating Authority in your state or territory beforehand for interstate boat license and boat operator requirements.

What about a personal watercraft or Jet Ski (PWC)?

Most states and territories require drivers of a personal watercraft or Jet Ski to be licensed. Sitting the test for your boat licence is only one step, but you will need to have a PWC endorsement to then drive a PWC. Be sure to check with the Maritime/Boating Authority in your state or territory beforehand for PWC licensing requirements.

Can I use an Australian boat licence overseas in the waters of another country?

It largely depends on the countries in which you intend to go boating. It is best to check directly with Maritime Authorities of each intended country of passage well in advance.

Can I use an overseas boat license in Australia?

If you have obtained a license in another country, but would like to go boating in Australian waters, generally speaking you will need to obtain the appropriate license locally for the Australian state or territory waters in which you will be boating. Some states and territories recognise international boat licenses for a period of time and others do not. Visit the state and territory links below for more detailed information.

Do I really need to get a boat licence?

In most cases the answer is YES, but this largely depends on the location, type and power of the boat you will skipper.

Captain's Briefing - Things to know

Consider this: Would you get behind the wheel of a car, for the first time in your life or in another country, and head straight out on the highway? Hopefully not!

The "rules and laws" of boating are very different to the rules of driving on the road in Australia. At the very least, it's important to understand these rules, for the safety of yourself, crew, and other boaters, and your boats. Grab your copy of the: Boat (PWC) Operator's Licence handbooks which are readily available for answers to this really good question. Ask your nearest Boat Dealer/Broker or your licencing authority or Boating Industry Association in your state or territory for your free copy, it's well worth the read and outlines all of the rules and laws of the waterways.

If you're just looking to drive a small boat and/or don't think you will need a licence it is still wise to get one. By attending a course and taking the subsequent licence test, you will learn lots of interesting and valuable information on safe boating, driving and navigation, which may save your life or someone else's.

Who is your local boating registration authority for registration and licensing purposes?

New South Wales
Maritime NSW   Ph: 13 12 56
www.maritime.nsw.gov.au

Victoria
Vic Roads   Ph: 13 11 77
www.vicroads.vic.gov.au

South Australia
Transport, Travel & Motoring   Ph: 13 10 84
www.sa.gov.au

Tasmania
Marine & Safety Tasmania Ph: 1300 135 513
www.mast.tas.gov.au

Queensland
Maritime Safety Queensland Ph: 07) 3120 7462
www.msq.qld.gov.au

Western Australia
Department of Transport Ph: 1300 362 416
www.transport.wa.gov.au

ACT
Recreational craft do not currently require registration
Boat licence requirements for the ACT are the same as NSW.

Northern Territory
Recreational craft do not currently require registration

Powerboat Handling Certificate

A wonderful initiative from the crew at Yachting Australia is their Powerboat Handling Course. An ideal way to receive the proper training required for safe boating with family and friends. For more information, visit: *www.yachting.org.au.*

Why not book into the course with the whole family!

Captain's Briefing - Things to know

The National Powerboat Handling Certificate

Overview | This course is aimed at people with a desire to own and/or be in charge of a recreational powerboat. The course covers the content of the Recreational Powerboat Operator Certificate, with added competencies drawn from the Sport and Recreation Training Australia Industry Training Advisory Board (SRTA ITAB).

Outcomes | You will gain the knowledge and skill to safely handle a recreational powerboat. You will also receive credit towards a Sport and Recreation Qualification and a Powerboat Handling certificate.
This course may be recognised for licensing purposes. Please consult your state or territory marine authority to see if this is the case.

Pre-requisites | This is an introductory course, so there are no pre-requisites

Where can I take the course? | Please contact a Yachting Australia Training Centre or your nearest Sailing Club. Please ask them about our Yachting Australia Logbooks so that you can monitor your progress.

What to do afterwards? | Continue training in Powerboat Handling to gain a Safety Boat Handling Certificate or Powerboat Handling Instructors Certificate

Honey, let's buy a BOAT!

SYLLABUS

1. Weather reports
- Interpret weather conditions from sources of information.

2. Plan and prepare a powerboat activity
- Comply with safety procedures when conducting maintenance.
- Demonstrate methods to remove vessels from the water and to haul and launch vessels to assist in slipping and launching vessels.
- Select suitable equipment.
- Prepare all equipment.
- Plan clothing requirements to the participants' needs and the length of the voyage.
- Plan provisions calculating the participants' usage and boat requirements, including water needs.

3. Operate a powerboat safely
- Identify and implement strategies to avoid unsafe practices when handling ropes.
- Correctly coil, stow and secure ropes to cleats and bollards, bits and Sampson posts.
- Determine and demonstrate the advantages and disadvantages of different hitches, bends and knots and use them appropriately.
- Identify the safety considerations related to the use of correct terminology on the powerboat.
- Anchor power boat in accordance with prevailing and forecasted conditions and legislation, rules and regulations.
- Identify the precautions and practices for overcoming potential dangers associated with getting under way and returning to berth.
- Identify specific tasks associated with getting under way and berthing when using different kinds of berth.

- Identify the affects of winds and current on maneuverability.
- Identify fire hazards on-board and fire prevention strategies.
- Determine search and rescue procedures, including drills used in the "person overboard" situation.

4. Operate engines
- Operate engines and craft to ensure safe handling during manoeuvering.

5. Perform a safe power boat activity
- Organise all the requirements for a safe power boating activity.
- Safely get underway, navigate a planned course and return to berth whilst complying with all related rules, regulations and legislation.
- Demonstrate power boat handling techniques while adopting minimal environmental impact practices.

6. Vessels knowledge
- Identify vessel design and construction features in order to determine the factors that affect safety, vessel stability and maintenance requirements.
- Maintain vessel stability through the implementation of procedures to reduce inadvertent movement of heavy loads and to reduce the amount of free water on decks/bilges and tanks.
- Determine the short and long-term maintenance requirements for particular vessels using knowledge of the materials used in hull construction.
- Implement general maintenance procedures for a vessel including maintenance of hull, rudder and stern gear, standing and running rigging and engine.
- Identify the location of safety equipment on-board the vessel.
- Demonstrate the correct use and stowage of safety equipment.
- Identify specific precautions necessary when making a coastal

passage in limited visibility and implement specific tasks as designated by the skipper.
- Implement methods to ensure personal safety in conditions of poor visibility, at night time and during heavy weather in accordance with operating procedures, including the use of life jackets, safety harnesses and lifelines.
- Demonstrate specific actions to be taken by crew for a person-overboard situation in coastal waters.
- Identify firefighting equipment for different types of fires and ensure such equipment is correctly stowed.
- Respond to distress situations in accordance with operating procedures, demonstrating correct care and use of emergency/safety equipment.

7. Working with the environment
- Identify the interrelationships occurring within a natural environment.
- Identify sources of environmental impact as related to the marine environment.
- Plan for minimal impact as related to the marine environment.
- Implement methods to minimise impact as related to the marine environment.

Who to contact:

Yachting Australia is located at:

Level 1, 22 Atchison Street,

St Leonards, Sydney, NSW 2065

Postal Address is:

Locked Bag 806, Milsons Point, NSW 2061

Captain's Briefing - Things to know

Phone (02) 8424 7400 and Fax (02) 9906 2366 for your nearest training centre.

www.yachting.org.au

Steps For Refuelling Your Boat

THIS SAFETY WARNING MUST READ BEFORE REFUELLING. REFUELLING YOUR BOAT IS DANGEROUS.

Before refuelling, if you have *any questions regarding* the safe operation of the fuel dock you are using, it's wise to speak to the operator or ask a competent mariner for assistance. Otherwise, if unsure of safe refuelling procedures or equipment use, we strongly advise you not to use the fuel dock or equipment.

The safety of you, your passengers and fellow mariners depends on this.

BEFORE REFUELLING

1. Read the refuelling instructions located at the bowser. If unsure, ask or do not use.
2. Do not smoke or strike any sparks in the area.
3. Read your vessel and engine manufacturer's operation manual for "Refuelling Instructions".
4. Turn engine(s) OFF, remove key(s) from ignition.
5. Disconnect all gas appliances and/or pilot lights.
6. Disconnect all electric power at main switch.
7. Close all hatches and the like, to prevent fuel from entering your bilge.
8. Turn ON your vessel's bilge blower.
9. All passengers to disembark and stand well-clear.

Captain's Briefing - Things to know

Before beginning the refuelling process, please observe the locations and operation of the:

- Fire equipment.
- All emergency fuel shut-offs.

Go to bowser and follow operation instructions.

Usually the filling of an approved fuel container meeting Australian standards is allowed, but remember to:

- Place the container well-clear of vessel and persons.
- Carefully monitor filling rate to avoid overfilling.

DURING REFUELLING

- Do not smoke or strike any sparks in the area.
- Maintain contact between hose nozzle and fixed pipe to prevent static sparks.
- Avoid any spillage onto the vessel or into the water.
- Carefully monitor filling rate to avoid overfilling.

AFTER REFUELLING

1. Do not smoke or strike any sparks in the area.
2. Hose down and clean-up all fuel filling points on your vessel and clean-up spillages.
3. Open all hatches to ventilate your vessel.
4. Check bilges for traces of fumes and/or spillages.
5. Adequately ventilate your engine(s) and fuel tank(s).
6. Allow fumes to evaporate and your engine(s) to be fully ventilated, before starting your engine(s).
7. Leave vessel bilge blower ON for a lengthy period of time into your journey.
8. Ensure your fuel cap is on tight.

Captain's Briefing - Things to know

9. Reconnect electrical and gas mains.

ONCE ALL PREVIOUS STEPS ARE FOLLOWED and WHEN COMPLETELY SATISFIED YOUR VESSEL IS FREE OF DANGER, THEN...

1. Insert key(s), then start engine(s).
2. Prepare vessel for departure (reconnect electrical and gas mains, secure hatches).
3. Ensure all passengers are wearing approved PFD's / Lifejackets (if required).
4. Passengers to board vessel.
5. Leave vessel bilge blower ON for a lengthy period of time into your journey.
6. Enjoy your time on the water.

The Boating Industries Alliance Australia is Australia's national peak body for the recreational and light commercial boating industry. It describes itself as "providing a national voice for the alliance of state Boating Industry Associations, including Western Australia, South Australia, Victoria, New South Wales, Northern Territory and Marine Queensland, working on their behalf as members to advance, promote and protect the boating industry". *www.biaa.com.au*

Boating Industries Alliance Australia

Marine House
300 Morphett Street
Adelaide SA 5000
PO Box 10083
Adelaide BC SA 5000
T   +61 8 8212 6207
E   info@biaa.com.au
W www.biaa.com.au
ABN 96 149 274 724

Your state Boating Industry Association (BIA)

New South Wales
Boating Industry Association of New South Wales
T: 02 9438 2077
E: info@bia.org.au
W: www.bia.org.au

Northern Territory
Boating Industry Association of Northern Territory
T: 08 8212 6207
E: office@darwinboatshow.com.au

South Australia
Boating Industry Association of South Australia
T: 08 8212 6000
E: info@boatingsa.com.au
W: www.boatingsa.com.au

Victoria
Boating Industry Association of Victoria
T: 03 8696 5600
E: info@biavic.com.au
W: www.biavic.com.au

Western Australia
Boating Industry Association of Western Australia
T: 08 9271 9688
E: admin@biawa.asn.au
W: www.biawa.com.au

Queensland
Marine Queensland
T: 07 3390 4657
E: info@marineqld.com.au
W: www.marineqld.com.au

Appendix D:

Captain's Log - Sample Forms
To make buying and selling easier

Statutory Declaration:

Australian law defines a statutory declaration as a written statement declared to be true in the presence of an authorised witness. The Statutory Declarations Act 1959 governs the use of statutory declarations in matters involving the law of the Australian Commonwealth, Australian Capital Territory, and other territories, but not including the Northern Territory.

Any person within the jurisdiction of this law may make a statutory declaration in relation to any matter. The declaration may be used in connection with matters of law, including judicial proceedings, but what weight is given to the declaration is a matter for the judge to decide.

Statutory declarations must be made in a prescribed form and witnessed by a person as specified in the Statutory Declarations Regulations (1993). Prescribed witnesses include legal and medical practitioners, Justices of the Peace, notary publics, police officers, military officers, registered members of certain professional organisations (i.e. National Tax Accountant's Association and Institution of Engineers Australia), and certain other Commonwealth employees.

Intentionally making a false statement as a statutory declaration is a crime equivalent to perjury, and punishable by fines and/or a prison sentence of up to 4 years.

Below is a Statutory Declaration that can be used to confirm that the seller of the boat and/or trailer is selling with clear title and that there are NO monies owing under a finance arrangement as discussed in earlier chapters on Buying a Boat and Selling a Boat.

TIP: The states of Australia each have their own laws regarding statutory declarations. This sample form can be used as a guide and I suggest you find out your local states requirements first and feel free to modify my form to suit.

Go to www.stkildaboatsales.com.au visit 'Sell Your Boat' to download your electronic copy of the Statutory Declaration.

Captain's Log -Sample Forms

STATUTORY DECLARATION

I, _____ of
_____ in the state of _____.
Do solemnly and sincerely declare that:
_____ is the sole owner of the following:

- _____ Vessel
  with Registration No: _____ and affixed with
  HIN: _____.

and

- _____ Trailer
  with Registration No: _____ and affixed with
  VIN: _____.

No other person, other than: _____
has any interest, legal or otherwise (including hire purchase, or leasehold interest) in the said Vessel and/or Trailer.

- The vessel is not encumbered by any mortgage charge, hire purchase agreement or other security.
- The vessel is not the subject of any current legal proceedings (threatened or actual) for the execution of any judgment debt.

AND I acknowledge that this statutory declaration is true and correct, and I make it in the belief that a person making a false declaration is liable to the penalties of perjury.

SIGNED x _____
          (vessel owner)
DECLARED AT _____
IN THE STATE OF _____ THIS _____ DAY OF _____ 20____
BEFORE ME _____
          (name of authorised person and capacity to witness)

SIGNED x _____ (witness signature)

On the coming into operation of the Magistrates' Court Act 1989, any of the following persons may witness the signing of a statutory declaration:

- A Notary Public
- A Justice of the Peace or Bail Justice
- A barrister and solicitor of the Supreme Court
- A clerk to a barrister and solicitor of the Supreme Court
- The Prothonotary or a deputy Prothonotary of the Supreme Court
- The Registrar or a deputy Registrar of the County Court
- The Principal Registrar of the Magistrates Court
- The Registrar of Probates or an Assistant Registrar of Probates
- The associate to a Judge of the Supreme Court or of the County Court
- The secretary of a Master of the Supreme Court or of the County Court
- A person registered as a patent attorney under Part XV of the Patents Act 1952 of the Commonwealth
- A member of the Police force
- The Sheriff or Deputy Sheriff
- A member or former member of either House of the Parliament of Victoria
- A member or former member of either House of the Parliament of the Commonwealth
- A councillor of a municipality
- A town clerk or shire secretary
- A legally qualified medical practitioner
- A dentist
- A veterinary surgeon
- A pharmacist

Captain's Log -Sample Forms

- A principal in the teaching service
- The manager of a bank
- A member of the Institute of Chartered Accountants in Australia
- A member of the Australian Society of Accountants or the National Institute of Accountants
- The secretary of a building society
- A minister of religion authorised to celebrate marriages
- A person who holds an office in the public service that is prescribed as an office to which this section applies
- A fellow of the Institute of Legal Executives (Victoria)

SAMPLE FORM
For the appointment of a Dealer/Broker
to sell your Boat and/or Trailer

Engagement Of Agent (Consignment / Brokerage Sale)

Engagement No: _____
Date: /   /

("The Agent")   _____
("The Owner")   _____
Address: _____
State: _____ Post Code:_____
Phone: H: _____ M: _____
Drivers Licence No: _____ Expiry: _____

The Owner desires to engage The Agent to sell the vessel during the agency period on the terms & conditions described within this engagement document.

Vessel: _____
Registration: _____ Vessel Name: _____
Year: _____ HIN: _____
Powered By: _____
Trailer: (if applicable) _____
Rgistration: _____ Year: _____ VIN: _____

Including: All fixtures, fittings, options and accessories as currently displayed on the vessel. The Owner will remove all personal effects, which are not included with the sale.
Minimum Acceptable Purchase Price Range
("the Minimum Acceptable Purchase Price Range")
Between $_____ **(Lowest) AND $** _____ **(Highest) inclusive of GST**
Commission Payable/Fee For Service: Per Clause No: 6A - 6B - 6C (strike out whichever is not applicable)
The Agency Period shall expire: Until the vessel is SOLD to The Owners satisfaction
(Inclusive and including any express or implied extension to this period.)

Type Of Agency: Sole and Exclusive or Non Exclusive, the listing to be shared with:

Special Conditions:

_____
_____
_____
_____

Encumbrances' or Liens:
Nil Finance to be sold with clear title OR under Finance/Liens with: _____
_____

Please Note: A Statutory declaration is also required outlining clear title/any other interests to the vessel.

I have read, understood and agree to be bound by the terms and conditions of this Engagement Of Agent (Consignment Sale) document. I agree to proceed as indicated.

*Engagement of Agency, Accepted by The Owner:

X _____ Date: /   /

*If not signed by the Owner, sign and print name of the Agent authorised to sign this agreement on behalf of the Owner

Engagement of Agency, Accepted by The Agent:

X _____ Date: /   /

Captain's Log -Sample Forms

Engagement No: _____

TERMS AND CONDITIONS OF AGENCY RELATIONSHIP

In consideration of _____ (The "Agent") using its best endeavours to sell the subject vessel, the Owner hereby grants to the Agent an agency for the vessel upon the following terms and conditions:

1. The Owner agrees to insure the vessel and to keep the vessel insured at all times for all risks and further agrees to indemnify and keep indemnified the Agent from all losses incurred by the Agent or claims made against the Agent in relation to the vessel or the Agent's use of the vessel in any way arising from or connected to this agreement.

2. The Owner grants the Agent authority to inspect and sea trial the vessel and otherwise to deal with or use the vessel as the Agent requires in order to sell the vessel.

3. The Owner warrants that the vessel is the Owner's vessel and that the Owner has the right and title to sell the vessel and that otherwise no impediment exists for the sale of the vessel.

4. The Owner agrees to supply a Statutory Declaration (see below) acknowledging that the vessel is unencumbered or stipulating any lien, encumbrance, or other parties that hold an interest in the vessel's ownership. (If a company) authorisation for the sale of an asset.

5. The Owner acknowledges that the vessel includes all fittings, fixtures and trailer (if applicable), unless noted on the face hereof.

6. **(a)** The Agent is hereby authorised to sell the vessel for a purchase price, which ensures that the Owner receives an amount within the Minimum Acceptable Purchase Price Range as the Owner's gross proceeds from the sale. This amount will be inclusive of any GST applicable. The Agent is hereby authorised to retain and is entitled to the difference between the actual purchase price and the (Lowest) Minimum Acceptable Purchase Price Range as the Agent's commission/fee for service on the sale. Regardless of the actual sell price, the minimum commission payable by the Owner under the terms of this Engagement is, _____ **Dollars.**

OR (Delete and Initial which payment method is not applicable)

(b) i> Percentage Calculation _____ Percent

of the actual purchase price within the Minimum Acceptable Purchase Price Range. The net figure, after the deduction of the agent's fee will be inclusive of any GST, which may be applicable to the Owner. Regardless of the actual sell price, the minimum commission payable by the Owner under the terms of this Engagement is, _____ Dollars

OR (Delete and Initial which payment method is not applicable)

(c) ii> **Agreed fixed amount** _____ **Dollars** of the actual purchase price within the Minimum Acceptable Purchase Price Range. The net figure, after the deduction of the agent's fee will be inclusive of any GST, which may be applicable to the Owner. Regardless of the actual sell price, the minimum commission payable by the Owner under the terms of this Engagement is, _____
Dollars.

7. The Agent will be entitled to a commission as agreed upon pursuant to this Agreement: -

(a) If during the agency period, the vessel is sold by the Agent, by any other Agent or by the Owner.

(b) If during a period of ninety (90) days after termination of this agreement the vessel is sold to a purchaser who is introduced to the vessel during the period of agency whether by virtue of a direct introduction to the vessel by the Agent or not.

8. The Agent is hereby authorised to pay any moneys owing to any other persons in relation to the vessel directly to such person from the proceeds of the sale particularly any moneys owing to persons holding encumbrances or liens notified on the face hereof.

9. All marketing and advertising fees or charges relating to the agreed sales campaign for this vessel are to be paid by the Agent as part of the agreement to sell. However, should the Owner elect to withdraw the vessel and/or trailer from sale prior to the expiration of the Agency Period, the Owner agrees to pay the Agent the sum of $_____ per calendar month incl gst, from the date of this agreement as reimbursement of marketing and advertising costs already undertaken and for future bookings made.

10. The Owner agrees that any moneys to be paid by any purchaser for the vessel during the term of this agency are to be paid to the agent and held by the agent pending the completion of any agreement with the purchaser and from

such moneys the Agent is entitled to deduct any commission and/or any other payments that are to be paid pursuant to this agreement, after which the Owner will be paid upon clearance of the purchaser's funds.

11. This Agency shall continue after expiration of the agency period until fourteen (14) days after receipt by the Agent of written notice from the Owner stating that the agreement is to be terminated.

12. In the event that this agreement is entered into by an agent of the Owner that agent warrants that the authority of the Owner is granted to the Agent to enter into this agreement on behalf of the Owner and that the Agent has the Owner's authority to bind the Owner to the terms and conditions as contained in this agreement. In this regard the agent of the Owner will provide _____ _____ ("The Agent"), any documentation that _____ ("The Agent") may reasonably require to be satisfied of the agent's appointment by the Owner.

13. The Owner releases and indemnifies the Agent, its servants and agents against (including the cost of defending or settling any action, claim or demand) which may be instituted against the Agent arising out of breach of this agreement by the Owner and/or as a result of defects or deficiencies in the goods supplied to the customer by the Agent on behalf of the Owner under this agreement.

14. Without limiting the provisions of Clause 12, the customer acknowledges and undertakes that it will meet all the costs of all actions, claims and demands of the customer as a result of defects or deficiencies in the goods provided to the customer.

I have read, understood and agree to be bound by the above terms and conditions of this Engagement Of Agent (Consignment Sale) document. I agree to proceed as indicated.

***Engagement of Agency, Accepted by The Owner:**

X _____ Date: /   /

*If not signed by the Owner, sign and print name of the Agent authorised to sign this agreement on behalf of the Owner

Engagement of Agency, Accepted by The Agent:

X _____ Date: /   /

Captain's Log -Sample Forms

SAMPLE FORM

VENDOR STATEMENT
(Victorian BIA members only. Other states please check)

BOATING INDUSTRY ASSOCIATION OF VICTORIA
VENDOR STATEMENT

Engagement Of Agent
Consignment / Brokerage Sale No: _____

Date: ___ / ___ / ___

Owner: _____

Address: _____

Suburb: _____ State: _____ P/C _____

Ownership

1. Are you the sole owner of the vessel?

☐ Yes ☐ No

2. If not, provide the name and contact details of any other person with a monetary or legal interest in the vessel.
_____
_____

3. Are you authorised to sell this vessel?
☐ Yes ☐ No

Registration

4. Is the vessel registered in your name?
☐ Yes ☐ No

5. If no, provide the name and contact details of the registered owner

_____

_____

Insurance

6. Is the vessel insured?
☐ Yes ☐ No

7. Which company is the vessel insured with?

_____

8. How much is the vessel insured for?

_____

9. What is your insurance policy number?

_____

Finance

10. Is the boat under finance?
☐ Yes ☐ No

11. If so, how much is owed on the vessel, and as at what effective date?

_____

12. Which company has provided the finance?

_____

Vessel condition and alterations

13. Is the vessel in good working order?
☐ Yes ☐ No

14. Has the vessel ever been involved in any accidents?
☐ Yes ☐ No

15. If so, please describe the damage and repairs.

_____
_____
_____
_____

Has the vessel been modified in any way?
☐ Yes ☐ No

If so, how has it been modified?
_____
_____

16. Is the engine powered within the manufacturer's specifications?
☐ Yes ☐ No

17. If your vessel is powered by a petrol inboard engine, is it fitted with an operating bilge blower?
☐ Yes ☐ No

18. When was the vessel last serviced and by whom?
_____
_____

19. Are service receipts available?
☐ Yes ☐ No

Usage

20. For what purposes have you used your vessel?
_____
_____

21. Does the safety equipment comply with current regulations and is it up-to-date?
_____
_____

Vendor must also provide:
- Copy of registration papers for vessel and trailer.
- Copies of service reports or contact details of service provider.
- Boat licence or drivers licence for ID.
- Certificate of currency for vessel insurance.
- Statutory declaration.

I have read, understood and answered the above questions in a truthful manner, to the best of my understanding.

I am comfortable to discuss the vessel history and my experiences of using this vessel on the water, with the buyer, if so requested.

Vessel Owner Name:
_____

Signed for and behalf of the vessel owner:

X _____

Capacity to sign: _____

Date: _____ / _____ / _____

Acknowledgements

Without the following people this book would not have been possible; given I repeated form 4 and was asked to leave school by the Principal at the end of form 5 to go "find a job" and "stop wasting everyone's time".

So for me to write this book offered many more challenges, much more than your average first-time author. My sincere thanks go to;

Andrew Rose - my business partner. Thanks for not questioning why I wanted to spend our money on this book project and on my personal development. Here's to both creating opportunity and building on our strengths and good reputation.

Key Person Of Influence (KPI) The 30 week entrepreneurial program has given me the framework, confidence and support to make this project real. To all of my KPI 2 colleagues, thank you for inspiring me, listening to me, supporting me and accepting me for the individual that I am.

Glen Carlson and Daniel Priestley - thank you for taking me on my incredible journey, one that I will never forget. Both you guys have a tremendous gift and may you long continue to challenge and question the norm, thereby extracting the gold from within!

Acknowledgements

Andrew Griffiths – My writing mentor and Australia's number 1 small-business author, presenter and advisor. You are a very caring person who keeps on giving and sharing. You're passionate about helping people to achieve their dreams and a truly inspiring role-model.

KPI accountability group – Keith, Jeremy, James and Geoff; I've truly loved the journey with you all, it's our differences that made us all work so well together as a team to each achieve great things. Geoff my program and book buddy - Hey mate we did it! Your honesty and gentle approach kept me focussed and on the track. I'll miss those daily emails.

Tim (Timbo) Reid - my long-time friend. Thanks for first suggesting I spend time doing some personal development. You all-but dragged me along to the KPI introduction seminar. I know it's hard putting up with your little buddy 'Delirious' for the past 20 years or so. Yes I'm very needy, yes I'm high maintenance, but I'm an author - so just get over it!

Mum, Dad, Debbie, Karen - I'll never forget that look on your face when I told you I was writing this book. It is always the same look you give when you're amazed and proud of my achievements. I love that look!

My in-laws (Ros & Hal) – Thanks for being Suzi's parents and always encouraging my ideas and plans. It all started because Hal suggested St Kilda Marina in the first place!

Little seeds do make big trees.

To my close-friends - who laughed at me when I said I'm writing a book. Who also remind me that I don't read books nor email and that I just look at the pictures! Surprise, Surprise -someone's got to set the benchmark of possibilities.

Transport Safety Victoria (TSV) – Janet Miller and Karin Limon
Club Marine Insurance – Greg Fisher, Ross Lambrick and Chris Beattie
Boating Industry Association of Victoria (BIAV) – Clyde Batty and Andy Warner

Acknowledgements

Don Finkelstein my proud Dad and devoted proof-reader
Andrew Fox
Richard Mollard
Body-builder, nephew, soon-to-be-lawyer and editorial assistant - Ryan Kornhauser
Geoff Green – GRG Momentum
Photographer extraordinaire - Gil Meydan
Quintrex – Cameron Wood
Boating Industry Alliance of Australia (BIAA)
Marine Queensland (MQ) - Don Jones
Streaker Boats – Leon and Paul Savage, Wayne Adolphson
Caribbean Boats – John Barbar and Richard Spooner
Ski Force Australia – Greg Chiminello
Cyberhorse - Bill
Parent Wellbeing – Jodie Benveniste
Jamie Ross
Hersh and Joel Burston
Anthony and Jodi Eden
Leon Rothman
Volvo Penta – Gavin Rooney
Mercury Marine – John Temple
Wally – Franco Mercatelli
Discover Boating USA – Carl Blackwell and Susan Lokaj
National Marine Manufacturers Association (NMMA) USA
Excite Books and Minuteman Press Prahran – Vivienne Kane

To all of you, a big thanks for your support of this project. Your assistance has been greatly appreciated.

Acknowledgements

May this book bring buyers and sellers into the marketplace to ensure the entire boating industry here in Australia grows and more people simply want to get onto the water!

A healthy and active boating community in Australia means everyone WINS.

References and Attributes

A big thank you to all of my valued sources.

Chapters 1 & 2
1. Interactive Schooling from: www.swirk.com.au
2. www.australia.com
3. www.businessdictionary.com
4. Discover Boating USA from: www.discoverboating.com
5. Jodie Benveniste from: www.parentwellbeing.com
6. Kerry McQueeny from: www.dailymail.co.uk
7. Richard Mollard
8. Australian Bureau of Statistics
9. Boating Industry Association of Victoria from: www.biavic.com.au

Chapter 3
1. Discover Boating USA from: www.discoverboating.com
2. www.google.com
3. National Marine Manufacturers Association (NMMA) USA
4. Boating Industry Association of Victoria
5. Marine Queensland from: www.marineqld.co.au
6. Streaker Boats from: www.streakerboats.com.au

Acknowledgements

7. Quintrex from: www.quintrex.com.au
8. St Kilda Boat Sales from: www.stkildaboatsales.com.au
9. International Marine, the makers of Caribbean Boats
10. MB Boats from: www.mbboats.com.au
11. Mercury Marine
12. Wally from: www.wally.com

Chapters 4 & 5

1. Discover Boating USA from: www.discoverboating.com
2. Boating Industry Association of Victoria (BIAV)
3. Marine Queensland from: www.marineqld.com.au
4. St Kilda Boat Sales from: www.stkildaboatsales.com.au
5. Mercury and Mercruiser from: www.mercurymarine.com
6. www.google.com
7. Volvo Penta from: www.volvopenta.com
8. Club Marine Insurance from: www.clubmarine.com.au
9. Club Marine Magazine

Chapter 6

1. Jodi & Anthony Eden
2. St Kilda Boat Sales from: www.stkildaboatsales.com.au
3. St Kilda Marina from: www.stkildamarina.net.au
4. Google images
5. Boating Industry Association of Victoria (BIAV)

Chapter 7

1. BoatSales / BoatPoint from: www.boatsales.com.au and www.boatpoint.com.au
2. St Kilda Boat Sales Service Centre from: www.stkildaboatsales.com.au

Acknowledgements

3. Boating Industry Association of Victoria (BIAV) from: www.biavic.com.au
4. Marine Queensland from: www.marineqld.com.au
5. www.wikipedia.com
6. www.sea-temperature.com
7. Transport Safety Victoria (Marine Safety Group) www.transportsafety.vic.gov.au
8. Club Marine Insurance from: www.clubmarine.com.au

Chapter 8

1. Discover Boating USA from: www.discoverboating.com
2. Boating Industry Association of Victoria (BIAV)
3. Marine Queensland from: www.marineqld.com.au
4. BoatPoint/BoatSales from: www.boatpoint.com.au
5. www.boatsales.com.au

Chapter 9

1. St Kilda Boat Sales from: www.stkildaboatsales.com.au
2. Boating Industry Association of Victoria (BIAV) from: www.biavic.com.au
3. Marine Queensland from: www.marineqld.com.au

Chapter 11

1. Discover Boating USA from: www.discoverboating.com
2. Boating Industry Association of Victoria (BIAV) from: www.biavic.com.au
3. Transport Safety Victoria (Marine Safety Group) www.transportsafety.vic.gov.au

Acknowledgements

Appendices

1. National Marine Safety Committee from: www.nmsc.gov.au
2. Boating Industry Association of Australia from: www.biaa.com.au
3. Transport Safety Victoria (Marine Safety Group) www.transportsafety.vic.gov.au
4. Boating Industry Association of Victoria (BIAV) from: www.biavic.com.au
5. St Kilda Boat Sales from: www.stkildaboatsales.com.au
6. Discover Boating USA from: www.discoverboating.com

About The Author

Darren Finkelstein is a long-time boatie, keen fisherman, slalom water-skier, author, entrepreneur, husband, father and a wanna-be pro surfer with very average ability.

Darren first started his business life working as a bank teller and quickly realised that a future in sales was better suited to his personality.

After spending many years in corporate IT with the likes of Fujitsu/ICL, Darren soon found his feet and true calling working for the innovators and deal makers at Apple for nearly 10 years, during the wonderfully inspiring Steve Jobs era.

Today, Darren, together with business partner Andrew Rose, are the co-owners of St Kilda Boat Sales and Service Centre, centrally located on the waters-edge at St Kilda Marina set amongst Australian finest boats and only 8kms from the Melbourne CBD.

What has now emerged is a boutique boat dealer that is truly unique because they focus on BOAT OWNERSHIP and not just selling boats.

Through the sale of power boats (both new and used) the guys service,

About The Author

repair, fuel and wash boats at the Marina. A true one-stop shop for all things marine, where a complete and pleasurable boat ownership experience - is the focus.

They service and repair over 300 boats per year at their accredited and fully equipped workshop employing only trained mechanics and marine experts. They are good guys, who have the can do attitude, minus the bull.

Their typical clientele are successfully self-employed, tradies, retirees and senior executives with some of Australia's largest companies.

Clients buy from Darren and Andrew because they give straight up advice; they feel safe and secure with a high level of comfort, which is why they trust them with the safety of their family on the water.

Thanks to their knowledge and expertise, they know what they are talking about and as a result they have literally sold hundreds of boats during their 10 years of operation. They are an industry accredited boat dealer and broker and have long term fuel contracts with the Water Police and Coast Guard.

Due to their intimate understanding of the marine industry, they quickly realised there were three key problems the market experienced:

1. Boat owners are time poor,
2. Owners don't have the required expertise to problem solve or
3. Clients want to deal with just one company, to do everything boating for them.

You can trust Darren, Andrew and their team to take the hassle out of boating. Their expertise takes all of the worry out of boat ownership, from the time you purchase your boat from them all the way until you decide to sell it with them again. This includes some friendly boat handling lessons as well as all the ongoing service and repairs that your boat requires. They will even wash and clean her regularly if you so desire!

About The Author

Never before has there been a better time to get on the water, sharing quality time with family and friends. It's all about lifestyle; you know that life is too short. So no more excuses!

Darren is currently on the Board of the Boating Industry Association of Victoria and Chairman of the Boat Dealer division. Darren has been elected by his fellow boat dealers in the state, for his third-term in office.

www.stkildaboatsales.com.au

Let's keep in touch

Here's how to get in contact with Darren Finkelstein

WEB
www.letsbuyaboat.com.au
www.stkildaboatsales.com.au

WRITE
Email: darren@stkildaboatsales.com.au
Fax: (03) 9525-5515

READ
Twitter: @thinkBoats
Facebook: darren.finkelstein
Facebook: stkildaboatsales
LinkedIn: Darren Finkelstein
Google+:   Darren Finkelstein

TALK
Darren's mobile: 0418-379 369
Skype: stkildaboatsales
International: +61 418-379 369
St Kilda Boat Sales: (03) 9525-5500
Service Centre :   (03) 9534-8213

WATCH
YouTube: stkildaboatsales

www.ingramcontent.com/pod-product-compliance
Lightning Source LLC
Chambersburg PA
CBHW051417290426
44109CB00016B/1332